What School is For

What School is For

Gabriel Chanan
and
Linda Gilchrist

Methuen & Co Ltd
11 New Fetter Lane
London EC4P 4EE

First published 1974 by Methuen & Co Ltd
11 New Fetter Lane, London EC4P 4EE
© 1974 Gabriel Chanan and Linda Gilchrist
Printed in Great Britain by
Richard Clay (The Chaucer Press) Limited
Bungay, Suffolk

ISBN hardbound 0 416 78510 7
ISBN paperback 0 416 78520 4

Contents

Acknowledgements   *page* vii

Chapter 1   The prospects for reform   1
*Behind the deschooling rhetoric; compulsory
education; technology and judgement; the
teacher's autonomy – myth and reality;
incoherence of the school; the viability of
reform; the uniqueness of schools; pressures
on the teacher; towards greater self-activity;
relationships among teachers*

Chapter 2   Formal and informal education   22
*No intellectual or cultural monopoly; the
need for teachers to listen; interaction
between formal and informal education*

Chapter 3   The pupils' culture   31
*Working class culture; pop music; teaching
as cultural synthesis; language; a pupils'
discussion*

Chapter 4   Middle class culture   48
    A phantom culture; 'the cultural heritage';
    dead culture or dormant culture?; the past as
    it was when it was the present; the present as
    the meaning of the past; education as
    intervention, not initiation

Chapter 5   Aims   71
    Manpower and knowledge; education for
    people's sake; goals for working class pupils;
    equality; the hidden potential of schools

Chapter 6   Curriculum structure   86
    Lessons and subjects; the gap between
    disciplines and lessons; the nature of
    concentration; the value of structure; fruitful
    deviations; focusing

Chapter 7   Selection and evaluation   105
    Uses of tests; IQ and ideology; testing of
    objectives; the test situation; context and
    limitations of testing

Chapter 8   Cultural revaluation   120

    Index   131

Acknowledgements

We would like to thank the many friends, teachers and others, who, knowingly or unknowingly, in agreement or disagreement, helped in the development of the ideas in this book. The names are too many to mention and the contributions too integral to define, but we hope they have fun trying to spot their bits.

Whatever you think, it's more than that.

Incredible String Band

The prospects for reform

BEHIND THE DESCHOOLING RHETORIC

Everything that could possibly be said against schools has probably been said by the deschoolers:[1] that they stifle curiosity, penalize initiative, destroy the will to learn; that they discriminate against the working class child, that they inculcate middle class values, that they foster competitiveness and discourage cooperativeness; that they perpetuate useless knowledge, that they erode critical awareness and reward mindless conformity.

Many of these points have substance. It is not our purpose to defend schools as they are. Yet the case for abolishing them is not proven. The hinted alternatives are very vague. Where they are at all specific they are indistinguishable from proposals for the *reform* of schools, not for an absence of schools. Where they do embrace the idea of abolishing schools, they show a strange faith in the educative capabilities of other agencies in the same society that created these schools, such as industry or the mass media. Ivan Illich's ingenuousness on this score is alarming:

The money now spent on the sacred paraphernalia of the school ritual could be freed to provide all citizens

with greater access to the real life of the city. Special
tax incentives could be granted to those who employed
children between the ages of eight and fourteen for a
couple of hours each day.[2]

Not only are children to go back into the factories when
schools are abolished, but the employers are to be paid by the
state – i.e. given even more control of the community's
wealth than they already have – for this great service to
education.

Schools are seen as the villains of the piece; if we only
let people interact spontaneously with their environment,
they would supposedly learn all they needed to know.
People do, of course, already interact with their environment, and learn an immense amount from it; and schools
are at fault in not recognizing this and redefining their
aims accordingly. Schools should teach what cannot easily
be learnt elsewhere. But the faults of schools are only one
source of society's problems. To criticize schools by contrast
with the organic educative capacities of society is to ignore
all the problems of society *other* than those embodied in the
school. It is, at root, an acceptance of that most conservative of educational aims – to enable the pupil to 'fit in with'
society.

Schools cannot stay as they are. We are only now on the
point of discovering how to use them so that they work.
The anomalies of traditional education – the learning which
was really parroting, the discipline which was really repres-
sion, the insistence on correct answers which was really
a rejection of independent thought – have been too
thoroughly exposed (by the criticisms of deschoolers among
others) to allow us to go back. Despite the shallow and
fumbling nature of some of the progressive educational
practices, there is no alternative to a thorough overhaul
of schooling.

There are a number of reasons to think that success is
possible, so long as we don't confuse the rationalization of
schooling with the saving of the entire society, to which
it is no more nor less than one major contribution. The

education system cannot solve society's problems for it. The problems of the education system partly reflect and partly influence those outside. It is realistic to aim to produce an education system that is *fit for* a socially progressive society at large, given that parallel efforts are going on in other sectors, without any illusion that education can bring about such a society on its own. The reforms one would like to see in education are thus neither superfluous nor apocalyptic in relation to social progress as a whole.

The parts of the deschoolers' case which are of value are those which, stripped of the rhetoric, actually concern reforms of schooling – i.e. the retention and development of the education system: lifelong, recurring education, possibly facilitated by a voucher system; schools to be used as community centres; imaginative use of technological equipment and audio-visual aids; a choice of subjects, institutions and learning styles; sympathetic adults to guide inquiry; and so on. Unless one is advocating total political and social upheaval – and the deschoolers say nothing of this – it is no more than a matter of semantics whether one speaks of abolishing the present education system and instituting another, or of radically reforming the existing one. Inflated rhetoric merely makes it harder to see what is actually being proposed. At the start of the essay just quoted,[3] Illich argues that there will shortly be an end to the age of schooling, and he distinguishes his 'aim to deschool society' from either 'transforming the world into a classroom' or 'establishing new free schools, independent of the system'. He then goes on to advocate the providing of 'institutions', 'a good educational system' and the exposure of children to 'confrontation or criticism by an experienced elder who really cares' (p. 74). A few pages later such people become 'professional personnel', and on page 83 it seems that they should be paid from 'public funds'. Finally we are told that the problem of what to do with the old, empty school buildings could be solved by giving them over to the new educational arrangements. Teachers paid by the state, working in the same buildings that used to be called schools – surely we have been here before?

Compulsory education

The only point on which there may be a vital difference
between deschoolers and plain reformers is the question of
compulsion, and here the deschoolers' lack of interest in
the classic class dilemma is a real weakness. In a voluntary
situation, the pressures against the working class child's
attending school (or community college) would be far
greater than those felt by the middle class child. Freedom
from school would mean earlier absorption into wage
slavery, ways being found to get around what laws against
this might remain. The deschooling argument, regarding
an earlier, closer encounter with industry as likely to be
truly educational, would excuse – indeed glorify – this
drift back to nineteenth-century conditions.

Industry would, of course, only teach people what it
wanted them to know. If industry took over the functions
of schooling, the faults of traditional schooling would
simply be instituted in a more inexorable, naked way : social
stratification, the inculcation of values of competition and
consumerism, a distorted emphasis on knowledge with a
rapid short-term application, and the discouragement of
independent critical thinking.

The argument that schools must now be abolished or
change their ways because 'working people will have to get
used to the idea of changing their occupations several times
during their lifetime'[4] is perfectly topsy-turvy. It assumes
that till now schools have been attempting to train people
for specific jobs, and that this was the source of their
educational limitations. Neither assumption is the case. Yet
they are just what would be the case if young people were
educated in factories.

The advantage of having special educational institutions
to mediate between society (including industry) and young
people is that these institutions can specialize in finding
the best level of *generalizable* knowledge – the kind of
knowledge which is transferable to the largest number of
different situations. This aim is implicit in the fact that
the school timetable is based on the structures of knowledge

– the academic disciplines – not the structures of employment. If we are concerned that people should be equipped, psychologically and in their skills, to do several different jobs, we are far more likely to get satisfaction from the traditional curriculum in some form, however rationalized and revaluated, than from closer connections with factories.

But if this is all that the aim of deschooling or progressive education amounts to, it is a miserably narrow aim compared even with that of traditional schooling, namely to equip a person with knowledge which will enable him to understand *any* situation. Of course, traditional schooling has failed in this aim, as far as most of the school population are concerned. But that is for reasons of its own, which we will shortly go into. We will never be able to evaluate this failure in a true perspective if we assume that the aim of education is to enable people to do a job, or even half a dozen jobs. The nature and conditions of work in our society are far more of a threat to the human spirit than schools are. The deschoolers are looking to a real tiger for salvation from a paper one.

Acquiring the ability to do a job is only one of a number of aims in education. In order to do an average working class job one needs very little formal education. Even in doing an average middle class job the ability to learn from the job itself and from those you work with, and the confidence that comes from status, responsibility and expectation, are probably more important than formal education. (The fact that there are many jobs which one cannot *get* without formal educational qualifications is a different matter.) Most jobs, mental or manual, do not draw on more than a fraction of the whole person, including his education, formal and informal, and his talents and interests. To educate people *for* jobs is to diminish them as human beings.

However, *to understand* one's job, to see its function in society as a whole, to know something of its scientific and historical background and of the legal and political developments that govern it – to know, in other words, far more than you strictly need to know in order to *do* the job –

is an aim more suitable to a true education. And to understand all this from the pivot of one's own working situation is to know also a great deal more that does not directly relate to one's work at all, but does relate to the breadth and depth of one's understanding of the world.

The aim of totally voluntary schooling is valuable as a long-term perspective, to be realized in conditions of much more general freedom of choice about one's life-activities. But a number of worthwhile reforms could be made in this direction while retaining the general framework of compulsory education. There should be options offered on a whole range of individual features of education : teachers, subjects, teaching styles, learning styles, times of attendance, schools attended – all could be gradually optionalized, subject only to practical considerations and some kind of common core course in basic essentials. Some form of permanent education should figure in this programme – a choice, that is, as to how one's allocation of educational time after the age of fifteen or sixteen should be distributed through one's adult life; with a built-in system of subsistence grants to counter the inevitable class difference in opportunities for making full use of one's allocation. All these possibilities are now on the agenda. Their value would be the impetus they gave to the struggle to make education more effective and attractive. Yet none requires or justifies the abolition of the general framework of compulsory education.

Nor does the incidence of truancy or of collective pupil rebelliousness. Both these important aspects of the educational scene argue for reform, not abolition. It was recently revealed[5] that an attendance figure of 88 per cent could mean that 54 per cent of a school's pupils were absent for one or more sessions a week. Many educationists reacted with alarm. But we find this possibility somewhat less alarming than that 12 per cent might have been absent for a whole week. For it simply means that half the pupils have been taking half a day off a week at different times, no doubt missing the lessons they liked least. This does not seem an unreasonable thing to do. If a half-day-off principle were accepted officially, it could no doubt be organized so as to disrupt courses as little as possible. This would be akin to the principle of 75 per cent attendance at lectures which is laid down at some universities, and it need not necessarily become the thin end of a wedge. It would simply make for a more tolerable general situation. As to the loss of learning time, this could not be mechanically calculated. Any reform which genuinely makes for a more tolerable and attractive learning situation will increase the effectiveness of learning overall, even if some percentage of available time is 'lost'.

Similarly the trend, if there is one, for greater collective pupil autonomy does not imply the breakdown of schools, even when it takes up an attitude hostile to school authorities. In fact quite the reverse. Psychologically speaking, collective activity within an institution represents acceptance of the collective identity conferred by that institution on its members, and creates greater internal cohesion, not less.[6]

Technology and judgement

In many respects, deschoolers merely give a radical gloss to some of the shallower assumptions of traditional schooling: that education is to enable people to get jobs – in which case why not have the factories teach the necessary skills directly? That education is to enable us to fit in with society – in which case what better than the direct encounter? A third such assumption is that education is primarily the provision of information – in which case it can be done better by computers.

The infatuation with technology is revealing. 'Tapes, retrieval systems, programmed instruction, and the reproduction of shapes and sounds tend to reduce the need for recourse to human teachers of many skills.'[7] But the providing of information was not what the teacher was there for in the first place, if he was any good. He does not teach merely information but how to *find* information, how to *structure* information, how to *coordinate* and how to *judge* information. If these more complex and more crucial

functions are ignored, the fantasy of an almost totally
mechanized education can reach rapturous heights.

> At the second and deeper level of interaction between
> student and computer programme, tutorial systems take
> over the main responsibility both for presenting a con-
> cept and for developing the skills necessary for its use....
> At the third and deepest level of interaction, dialogue
> systems are aimed at permitting the student to conduct a
> genuine dialogue with the computer.[8]

A *genuine* dialogue would surely imply that the computer
has become human. Since this is not possible, perhaps what
is really meant is that the human being will become a
machine.

The advantage of the encounter is supposed to be that
learning can be totally tailored to the individual. Here
again is the uncritical acceptance of the traditional assumption that learning is essentially an encounter between the
private mind and 'knowledge', not an encounter between
human beings. If totally individualized learning ever came
about it would be a nightmare of isolation from the social
stimuli to learning, including pupil-pupil and pupil-teacher
interaction. The traditional attempt to separate pupils from
each other in order to 'make them get on with their own
work' is here taken to its logical conclusion.

The emphasis put on the technological component is in
any case spurious. Paradoxically it seems to be educationists
who, more or less following McLuhan, object to the 'pri-
vatism' and 'linear thinking' of books who are most easily
infatuated with information systems which are far more
isolating, linear, cumbersome and inflexible than books –
and yet which, of course, derive any cogency they may have
from their dependence on books. Computer programmes are
invented by people and are therefore as fallible as people
are – but nothing like as flexible in changing course or
correcting mistakes. To attempt to computerize teaching
functions other than the simplest is to risk institutionaliz-
ing errors and shortcomings on a magnificent scale.

This misidentification of understanding with having

access to information is precisely one of the most limiting features of traditional education. The crucial skills which teachers pass on are those concerned with the manipulation of symbolic structures, i.e. the systems that permit comparison, development and judgement. Technological aids are useful at certain stages to augment the fundamentally human encounter. But they can never supersede teachers because they cannot reproduce *judgement*. And they cannot supersede the written word because they are dependent on the written word for the devising of their own programmes.

THE TEACHER'S AUTONOMY – MYTH AND REALITY

Our main concern in this book is with the educational prospects for working class pupils, and with the teacher of working class pupils in the secondary school. All our examples are from the British education system, but the principles are likely to be universally applicable in one degree or another. Though we address ourselves primarily to teachers –and most of the ideas in this book have come from teachers – we hope also to be overheard by others who have any influence or potential influence on the schools. Much of the time we will unavoidably seem to be saying what we think teachers 'ought' to do, when what we really mean is what they ought to be *enabled* to do. Teachers are often enough eager to do what they ought, and are perhaps the only ones who really understand what it is; but circumstances in and out of school impede them. The belief in individual teacher autonomy is convenient for educationists. But if education is not a panacea for the whole society it is nevertheless a product of the whole society. The teacher alone cannot solve the teacher's problems.

Those who are concerned that genuine advances in universal education should emerge from the present turmoil in schools will make it a priority to *relieve* pressures on teachers, rather than simply urge more and more practices upon them, so that they can become more genuinely autonomous and capable of orchestrating the necessary reforms. There can be little serious progress while our education system is stratified in such a way that the teachers of pupils who have the greatest needs and difficulties are given least time, resources and reward to support their work.

The lip-service paid, in the British system, to the individual teacher's right to do what he thinks best in his own classroom is a symptom of contradiction. For it is barely possible for a teacher to make sense and success of his objectives when he is working within a situation which is determined in all sorts of ways by factors over which he has no control. By comparison with most other state education systems, British schools and classrooms are very diverse. This is indeed a valuable freedom. But best use can be made of it only when the surrounding constraints are appreciated.

Incoherence of the school

We do not share the view of some radicals who would suggest that the teacher's autonomy is a complete myth since the schools are ruling class institutions dictating the values that are to be put across. But we do believe that the constraints on the teacher's work are much greater than the conventional educational wisdom would suggest, and that they do, in their muddled way, promote social conservatism and educational feebleness more than social equality and educational effectiveness. That we must comply with constraints and demands does not mean that these have been systematically worked out by the ruling class. The contours of a 'ruling' ideology appear through the convergence of a great variety of ideas which have in common only that someone thought of each that it would justify or defend some established interest. Ruling classes are rarely as rational as they would be if they had been designed by Marxists. They are not always sure what their longer-term interests are nor how they are best served. Hence the endless debate surrounding education is not incompatible with a feeling of vacuum or bewilderment within it – a feeling that no-one knows exactly what the goals are or can give firm guidance, though everyone is clamouring for particular interests to be served.

Bewilderment is a thing which institutions do not acknowledge. You will not hear a headmaster or the principal of a college say publicly 'We don't know what we're doing' nor even 'We have doubts about what we're doing.' What you will hear are plenty of vague assertions about the way forward, the development of pupils' potential, the pursuit of excellence, the maintaining of standards and so on, and plenty of particular decisions on particular rules and practices.

Bewilderment and doubt are central experiences in most people's lives, particularly in a society which embraces a great variety of attitudes and beliefs. But where there is no common acknowledgement of bewilderment the individual may feel that it is all his own. This is a particular hazard for the teacher, in his psychological isolation. Teachers in the staffroom rarely feel they can discuss what went wrong with a lesson, other than in terms of pupils' shortcomings. Yet without such openness how can teachers begin to work together to make schools into places which make sense to pupils?

A great deal of teacher education and theory consists in urging the individual teacher to adopt this or that attitude or practice, whether a child-centred approach, curriculum planning, objective evaluation or whatever. Very little is done to prepare him for the far-from-propitious circumstances in which he is to put these practices into effect. These circumstances might often include the hostility of other, more established teachers to some of the innovations; a lack of suitable equipment and textbooks; a school atmosphere which is the opposite of child-centred; lack of adequate time for the analysis and planning of objectives; subjection to the decisions of a headmaster or head or department who does not share these aims; and confrontation with a body of pupils whose expectations and behaviour have been shaped by repressive or discouraging teaching from others. For the individual young teacher to attempt to introduce educational reforms recommended by his training into a situation like this is to put himself under a far greater strain than simply the strain of 'teaching', itself notorious enough. His training forgot to tell him that the protection of his own well-being and sanity are prerequisites for any capacity he may have to contribute to improvements in schools.

A training which does not prepare teachers for the incoherence of the average secondary school as a learning environment is something of an evasion. A training which encourages the missionary spirit but does not equip the novice for conflict and tension is something of a contradiction. 'In the course of qualifying', we are advised,[9] 'a teacher must at one and the same time acquire a dual capacity which means fitting in with schools as they are, but in addition developing an independent and critical perspective which will ensure that future possibilities for progress are not neglected.' This makes the future possibilities sound like some impersonal beneficent process which will begin without the teacher's active help. But how are such possibilities for progress even to come onto the agenda if not through the efforts of the teacher himself? And if through the teacher then in some respects at least his main asset is that he does *not* fit in with the schools as they are.

In reality the aim of 'fitting in with schools as they are', like the aim of fitting in with society 'as it is', is not viable, for it unjustifiably implies a coherent status quo which can be either accepted or resisted as a whole. But since the status quo is not static but is itself a state of tension and conflict, only a very superficial participant could appear to be fitting in with it.

The problems of the individual teacher, in classroom and staffroom, are part of a large social pattern which he cannot hope to resolve on his own. The difficulty in getting his message across, the difficulty of establishing fruitful relationships with his pupils, the tension between what he teaches and what is examined – these and scores of other difficulties are not accidents of the individual teaching situation. Whatever can be done to improve the situation and solve these problems will need the concerted effort of groups of teachers together if it is to have a chance of success.

THE VIABILITY OF REFORM

The uniqueness of schools

The rationalization of secondary education is only just beginning. The potential of a progressive school system, as opposed to a sprinkling of progressive practices within a still predominantly traditional system, has not yet been discovered.

On the level of generalized criticism, it is worth distinguishing between the deschoolers' criticisms of schools as bad in themselves, a *source* of social ill, and left-wing criticism of schools as a faithful *reflection* of ills stemming from society at large, specifically its economic organization.

It is precisely because schools reflect the pressure of other ills in society that it does not make sense to regard them as *the* villains of the piece. But neither are they *merely* a channel for society's other faults. There is no particular immutability in the way they have crystallized thus far, no reason for thinking that they could not be radically changed short of a revolution. For whether you regard the present state of society as exemplary, tolerable or utterly execrable, the schools are not a faithful reflection of it. Look at the specific characteristics of schools and compare them with the equivalent features of society as a whole. The way that rules are made and enforced in the school is nothing like the way that laws are made and enforced in society. The role of a headmaster is not like that of a prime minister, who is elected and open to public criticism, nor of a company director, who rarely orders or disciplines workers directly, nor of a foreman, who is in continual direct contact with the workers in the working situation. The school timetable is utterly unlike the structure of the working day in any other institution. The psychology of the teacher, with all the influences that help to shape it, is distinct from the psychology of any other kind of worker. The school 'culture' – the prefect system, the house system, the morning assembly, prizegivings and speechdays, school songs, rules and so on – is a concoction unlike anything else in society, a *sui generis* synthesis of all sorts of influences, markedly different in feeling from the culture of society at large, either popular or highbrow.

Finally, schools are decisively different from industrial institutions (for which left-wing critics sometimes see them as antechambers) in the respect that all activities in industry are measured by the clear (if unhealthy) motive of profit. There is no comparable criterion of success in the education system, healthy or otherwise. There are exams, but the aim of the system is not to maximize exam results, which are arbitrated from within the system itself. There has to be a large, controlled failure rate for the exams to work as they do. The success of the exams themselves means the failure of most of the pupils. Most real success and failure in teaching goes unregistered, and the education system hardly recognizes it as a criterion.

We are not saying that the school is unrelated to the rest of society. On the contrary, it is related in multiple ways, almost beyond disentangling. But its nature is not discoverable by general analogies with any other particular institution, nor with society as a whole. Its potentialities, within a society that is itself changing, are unknown. We can, of course, anticipate resistance to changes. But we cannot know beforehand what the limits of our success in overcoming that resistance will be – unless we abandon the attempt right here.

The apparent inertia in schools, their capacity to absorb good intentions, young idealisms, fertile new ideas like cotton wool and still remain essentially the same places, is no proof of their fundamental unchangeability, for scores of reforms are urged upon them at once from different quarters and with different justifications. The quiet cancelling out of many of these pressures, the failure of theorists, policymakers or teachers collectively to *coordinate* reforms means that, in effect, the big push has not yet been tried.

PRESSURES ON THE TEACHER

The single most important reform that could be made in

schools in the short term would be the designation of one day a week in term time for every teacher to participate in planning and collective assessment of their work. The reason why so many promising ideas fail to come to fruition is that teachers are always living from day to day, from lesson to lesson. There is little time or provision for the reading, discussing and planning that would be necessary if serious reforms were to be put into effect. Teachers in universities, working with tiny, highly motivated student groups, have relatively few contact hours and large periods of time for reading and preparation. Teachers in secondary schools, with large, disaffected pupil groups, have long contact hours and piles of marking. They have *more* reading to do to keep up with their subject than university teachers do, because there are both advances in the subject and advances in the pedagogy of the subject to be absorbed. At university, the first level suffices for both. Contrary to popular impressions, the teacher works long hours even when holidays are taken into account.[10] It is not surprising, then, that teachers have little time to devote to educational theory beyond their own subject. The organization of teachers' work makes, in fact, no provision even for keeping up with their own subject. It seems to be assumed that teachers will spend their entire careers drawing on their three or four years of specialist education over and over again – and this, of course, is what often happens. Provisions for increases in in-service training[11] will do some good, but not as much as would be done by the institution of a weekly planning day. Teachers do not need more and more good advice, some of which will not be good, some of which will be too vague to be useful, some of which will be jargonized and baffling (for we can assume that in-service courses will suffer from the same content-problems as initial training). They need more support in the developing and implementing of their own ideas within the working situation of which only they know the full complexity. We are not arguing for time in which teachers can be subjected to what now passes for theory in the colleges, but for time to work out principles for themselves, drawing on whatever expertise they find helpful.

The provision of a weekly planning day would not need a full 20 per cent increase in the teacher salary bill. The logic of progressive education is towards greater self-activity on the pupils' part. The conventional musical-chairs time-table is based on an assumption of a norm of pupil passivity and recalcitrance. Pupils have to be told what to do; they cannot be trusted; they do not want to learn; they have to be made to learn : this involves imposed discipline; they don't like discipline and are liable to rebel : they therefore need constant supervision. Professing to cope with this situation, the timetable exacerbates it. Sustained concentration, rhythmic development of learning to a natural climax, is impossible. At the sound of a bell everything must change – the room, the subject, the teacher, sometimes the group. Half the energy of every lesson is taken up by the attempt to establish borders, procedures, norms for an arbitrary unit which will be abandoned again in a few moments. The overriding criterion of timetable planning is to make sure that all classes are occupied in all contact hours. The effect of adjacent lessons on each other, the effect of the cumulative sequence of lessons, is not considered. The need for balance between different types of concentration, between listening and doing, between absorbing and creating, between accommodation and assimilation, is unconsidered. The overall effect is an imposed superficiality, a self-fulfilling prophecy of pupil passivity, uninvolvement, restlessness and all that follows. And one of the things that follows is that there is no let-up in the sequence of demands made on the teacher's energies.

TOWARDS GREATER SELF-ACTIVITY

Although it would be difficult to devise a blueprint, it would not be difficult to imagine a different arrangement. One of the major elements in it would be considerable periods allocated to pupils' self-organized activities within a general framework of teacher consultation. Part of the school environment would be reorganized as resource centres, supervised as necessary: quiet rooms, discussion rooms, audio-visual equipment rooms, teacher consulting rooms, and so on. A main objective of courses in the first years at secondary school would be to socialize pupils into relatively autonomous activity. And there would be a net gain of teacher time salvaged from former contact hours, to be devoted to the planning, discussion and evaluation necessary to the entire arrangement and other concomitant reforms.

A means of achieving this pattern by stages would be to start by designating the last lesson of each day as a period in which pupil clubs and societies could operate, in the way they already do at lunchtimes, but on a more ambitious scale.

Possible objections of 'not covering the syllabus' would have to be weighed against the self-defeating nature of the present timetable and against the change towards more pupil-oriented objectives which would probably be occurring at the same time. If pupils could actually learn how to learn instead of having to try and learn only what they are told, the syllabus would be 'covered' ten times more fully.

There is a further point that is vital but difficult to get across because, on the surface, it runs counter to some progressive assumptions: it is that the liberalizing of the timetable and of relations between teachers and pupils, and the introduction of some measure of choice as to which lessons are attended, is fully compatible with *more* highly structured lessons some of the time.

It is always difficult to get across the fact that the best combination of reforms is not necessarily the conjunction of a number of reforms all conforming to some similar principle, such as greater integration or child-centredness. Since the traditional school has been a school mechanically compartmentalized in so many respects, the principle of greater integration does indeed recur in many progressive reforms: greater integration between subjects, teachers' work, ability groups, and so on. But 'underlying principles' are almost always polar extremes which make sense only

in relation to their equally abstract opposites. It would be
absurd to base any educational policy on integration alone.
Differentiation must also be considered, and the best policy
will be the best balance or interaction between the two
(which does not necessarily mean the best *compromise*). In
the present case, the greater the degree of choice that pupils
may have as to whether or not they go to a particular
lesson, and the greater the equality of social relationship
between teachers and pupils, the greater the viability and
desirability of having *some* highly structured, highly
teacher-directed courses on offer as part of the spectrum of
options. If they proved highly popular, this would not necessarily be regressive. Since the package as a whole is not being
forced down anybody's throat, pupils will be able to orien-
tate more positively to closely guided learning opportunities
as to other modes. For comparison, art and entertainment in
society are wholly voluntary activities, yet most packages
are highly structured and directed. While this corresponds
in many cases to a norm of audience passivity, it would be
absurd to say that it did so in all or even most cases, for
concentrated appreciation, when it is genuinely occurring,
is a highly active experience even though it engages with
a highly prestructured work of art. Certain kinds of intense
imaginative or intellectual experience are attainable only
through thorough prestructuring by the presenter.

The resistance to teacher-directed lessons has sprung partly
from the fact that they are often very *poorly* structured,
and partly from the fact that, in the traditional school, the
teacher's right to tell you what to do, which is essentially a
social, not an intellectual imposition, is not distinguished
from his claim to know more. Resistance to the one therefore automatically entails resistance to the other. But if the
genuine offence, the social imposition, is attenuated, the
genuine – intellectual – authority can be accepted where
it is trusted or found to be convincing. This does not mean
that fruitful leads by pupils would not be followed on such
courses (see chapter 6 below).

RELATIONSHIPS AMONG TEACHERS

Finally, it must be recognized that a key development necessary to serious reform in schools is the development of collective staffroom consciousness; not so much in the sense of formal democratic procedures[12] such as representatives on boards of governors, though these might or might not be found helpful, but in the sense of understandings and strategies worked out by a widening circle of allies who share progressive educational aims.[13] Both the practical and the psychological situation of staffrooms cries out for something of this kind. No headmaster, however progressive and efficient he may be, could know all that must be known in order to guide a community through changes of this complexity. Every teacher has unique access to part of the evidence from which the overall picture must be built; every teacher must therefore have the opportunity to influence all. Democratic participation does not come naturally to the traditional teacher, isolated in so many ways, yet it would bring him possibly more relief than he can yet imagine. Only when relationships among teachers become more open and mutually supportive will they feel sufficiently secure to enter into the more equal relationships with pupils on which effective teaching vitally depends.[14]

NOTES

[1] The best known advocate of deschooling is Ivan Illich. Recent essays by him and others of a similar persuasion are to be found in Bruce Rusk (ed.), *Alternatives in Education* (London, University of London Press, 1972); and in Peter Buckman (ed.), *Education Without Schools* (London, Souvenir Press, 1973). A round-up of anti-school arguments is made in section 2 of *The Free School* by Kenneth Richmond (London, Methuen, 1973).

[2] Ivan Illich, 'The de-schooling of society' in Rusk, op. cit.

[3] Ibid, pp. 71-2.

⁴ Buckman, op. cit., Introduction, p. 3.

⁵ Anonymous, 'Truancy: what the official figures don't show', *Where*, 83 (August 1973) (published by the Advisory Centre for Education).

⁶ The recently rediscovered schoolchildren's strikes of 1911 make interesting comparisons with recent events, and give an indication of what generation upon generation of school pupils must have felt. The demands were for various measures that would make schools more tolerable places, not for the abolition of schools. See Dave Marson, *Children's Strikes in 1911* (Oxford, Ruskin College History Workshop Pamphlets, No. 9, 1973).

⁷ Ivan Illich in Rusk, op. cit., p. 85.

⁸ Patrick Suppes, 'Alternatives through computers' in Rusk, op. cit., p. 33.

⁹ Doris M. Lee, 'Perspectives in the education of teachers', *Bulletin* of the University of London Institute of Education, New Series No. 17 (Spring Term 1969), p. 7.

¹⁰ See S. Hilsum, *The Teacher At Work* (Slough, National Foundation for Educational Research, 1972).

¹¹ As forecast by Department of Education and Science (Great Britain), *Education: A Framework for Expansion* (white paper) (London, HMSO, 1972).

¹² The dangers of formal democratic participation in an essentially undemocratic education system are discussed in A. E. Jenning, *The Struggle in Education* (London, IMG Publications (182 Pentonville Road, London N.1), 1973). This is a reply to *Democracy in Schools*, published by Rank and File (see note 13 below) in 1971 (86 Mountgrove Road, London, N.5).

¹³ The nearest thing to this at present existing with a formal organization is the Rank and File teachers' group. However, its attitude to the possibility of school reform is ambivalent and it would be unlikely as a body to espouse all the reforms proposed here.

[14] For fuller treatment of this issue see Arnold Downes, 'Relationships among teachers' in Douglas Holley (ed.), *Education and Social Domination* (provisional title), London, Hutchinson (in press).

NO INTELLECTUAL OR CULTURAL MONOPOLY

A great deal of discussion about educational objectives fails to make clear whether and when one is talking of education in the broad sense, as an activity that goes on spasmodically in almost any human intercourse, and when of education in the sense of that which is carried out in the education system. Our concern is to find the right goals for *schools* to adopt. These cannot be based on the assumption that the education system has a virtual monopoly of society's intellectual activity. The crucial question is what is the relationship between the living education received spasmodically from society and the organized education received systematically from the school.

There has been mounting proof over the last decade and longer of the strong influence of the home on school attainment. But these findings have not prompted any serious appraisal of the intrinsic content and value of out-of-school education. Interest has only been shown in what goes on outside school as a factor influencing capacity to succeed inside school. Yet the fact that the relation of middle class children's out-of-school education to their in-school education is stronger than that of working class children tells us nothing about the intrinsic value of either.

Even the more forward-looking of assaults on the problem of educational objectives often fail to tackle the question of what the content of society's informal education is, and what relationship formal education ought to hold to this. As a result, schemes of objectives intended for schools are attempts at breakdowns of the total content of given subject areas. Though this does not strictly imply that the pupil's mind is initially empty, it has the effect of bolstering this belief – a belief supposed to have disappeared from educational thought long ago. There is an assumption that formal education is the ultimate source of all worthwhile knowledge.

The danger in this assumption is that it leads to a systematic underestimation of pupils' mental resources – not only their intrinsic creative potential but the content of the culture or subculture which they have already internalized. The problem of recognizing the nature and value of what is already in the pupil's mind is not adequately solved by tests which measure the stage of a pupil's attainment in a school subject, because what is at issue is precisely the question of whether school education represents (and represents accurately) the total mental content of society or whether there are other kinds of knowledge which it does not cover.

The identity of the pupil is formed primarily out of school by some synthesis of his native creativity, the language habits and culture of his home background, and the influence of mass media, peer groups and so on. For the school to fail to recognize this cultural synthesis as the basis of any further learning is to fail to recognize the identity of the pupil. This failure prevents the success of formal education in two separate ways: first, in its effect on the psychology of the pupil, in that it negates the only basis on which he can internalize the new concepts, values and experiences offered him by the school; second, by leaving the teachers in ignorance of what is really in the pupils' minds, so that they are unable to select suitable material and pitch their objectives at the right level.

Many teachers would claim that they already knew what the content of the pupil's native culture and state of mind was. It is easy to see, for example, that at certain ages there are salient preoccupations with sex and violence. But in any other situation it would seem, on the face of it, an extraordinary claim that one knew in any depth the content of the minds of any group of thirty people with whom one came into contact only in an institutional situation for brief periods three or four times a week.

A preoccupation with sex and violence does not, on its own, tell us very much. After all, vast sections of traditional culture are preoccupied with sex and violence, under the titles of love and death. If great art is a sublimation of eternal human fears and wishes about love and death, how could one expect other than to find these preoccupations in a raw form in the adolescent? If we think that the culture we wish the pupils to accept offers them better ways of dealing with these preoccupations than they have at their disposal already, clearly we must accept the legitimacy of these preoccupations in their raw form in the first place. This does not mean that we ought to accept the legitimacy of violence – quite the reverse. But we deny the pupils real access to whatever may be of value in formal culture if we present it as something unrelated to their own preoccupations instead of, as it is in fact, related to them in the profoundest possible way.

THE NEED FOR TEACHERS TO LISTEN

Our image of the teacher is still of one who stands up and holds forth – one who *initiates* what is to be learned and only asks questions in order to discover if what he has presented has been absorbed. The whole classroom conversation is held on terms controlled by him. Two-thirds of all classroom talk is done by teachers.[1] In some primary schools there is still a 'rule of silence' – thus ensuring that teachers have to spend most of their time reprimanding and punishing pupils. The skill of listening is as yet hardly recognized as vital for teaching, even though we all know that it forms a good half of satisfactory communication with our friends. In the teaching situation, where there is likely to be a much wider gap between assumptions and reference points (of teacher and pupils) one would expect that a great deal more listening was necessary on the part of the teacher, as well as a great deal more tailoring of the things he said to the concepts already demonstrated by the pupils.

Thus the need for listening is justified purely on grounds of teaching technique. But there are also deeper questions at issue here, and these concern the nature of the autonomous content of the minds of, say, working class adolescents. To many teachers this appears as such a threatening area that it seems to bear no relation at all to the 'safe' concepts and values which they see themselves as trying to teach. It is undoubtedly a very problematic area, and as much so for the egalitarian teacher as for the conservative; for while the egalitarian teacher might not be disturbed by adolescent tastes in music, clothes, entertainment, slang and sex, he cannot contemplate violence, racism and intolerance with the same equanimity.

The crucial question is not whether the school should *condone* the culture of its pupils but whether and how it can *relate* to it. The 'culture' of an adolescent group is in any case likely to be in a highly volatile state, so that condoning it, if it could be pinned down at all, would be condoning something which the adolescents themselves might be criticizing before the year was out. (The culture of their parents would of course be more stable, though not static.) Until we have made some space for the pupils' self-expression we cannot really know *who* our pupils are; and cannot therefore have much idea of the meaning to them of the concepts we are purveying.

The value of talk is much greater than merely the information which it gives the teacher, though that is our main point here. Barnes, Britton and Rosen[2] provide many valuable illustrations of pupils' talk. The main point to be endorsed is that it is by talking (and writing) that pupils learn. Talking is not merely the expression of stored concepts – it is the effort of conceptualization in action. And collective discussion is of course a multiple interaction of this process. But the skills of restraint, empathy and drawing out are probably even more difficult than those of holding forth interestingly. The Schools Council Humanities Project[3] is based on fostering collective classroom discussion: every teacher who has used this technique knows that it requires at least as much teaching skill to foster discussion as it does to monopolize it – and a good deal more personal confidence.

There is also the question of what *sorts* of talk are encouraged. The traditional teacher frequently recognizes and endorses nothing outside

> the effort on the part of the pupils to guess almost the very form of words the teacher has in mind.... The teacher's carefully composed structuring and soliciting moves, whatever their advantages, have the disadvantages of tightly circumscribing the extent to which a pupil can formulate and represent in words what he is thinking[4]

– or trying to think.

It is only after this claustrophobic situation has been transcended that one can begin to judge with any sense of realism firstly the nature of the pupils' intrinsic efforts to grasp reality and secondly what function structured subject matter could have for them. The best role for formal education is the one that best interacts, both critically and complementarily, not only with the pupil's own creativity but with the particular synthesis of influences which makes up his culture.

INTERACTION BETWEEN FORMAL AND INFORMAL EDUCATION

Rather than plunge into debate about the relative virtues of middle class and working class culture (terms to which we address ourselves in the succeeding chapters) we have

started by making a straightforward distinction between
what is learned inside and outside the school. Informal education cannot decisively be divided into working class and
middle class components, because these elements are in
flux, constantly acting and reacting on each other. It makes
more sense to start by noting that some of the elements of
contemporary culture are highly centralized while the
origin of others is more diffuse. Centralized structures such
as law, the church, the armed forces, television, cinema,
press, publishing and advertising all educate; and so also
do diffuse phenomena like ordinary talk, jokes, shop floor
militancy, privately held values, family relationships and
peer group subcultures. So indeed do such part-diffuse, part-
centralized pursuits as trade unionism, fashion in clothes,
the arts, entertainment and sport.

Thus we are not concerned here only with anything that
might lay claim to being an independent working class
culture; we are concerned with the educational effects in
the broad sense of every agency in society outside the school.
Both the highly centralized agencies, ultimately directed by
a small minority of people highly placed in society, and the
diffuse, reflecting the autonomous influence of wider groups
of people, furnish living elements of the pupils' consciousness. From these elements each individual fashions the
store of behaviour models, moral and aesthetic touchstones,
criteria of action and reference points of meaning that he
carries around in his head. These are not passively ingested,
and are not fixed once and for all, but are creatively syn-
thesized, and the synthesis is either recharged or revised
at each encounter with new works of art or entertainment,
other people's values, public customs, laws and institutions.
Thus what matters about traditional schooling's neglect
of or hostility towards contemporary culture is not that it
has been a sin against contemporary culture (which is fairly
impervious to such offences) but that it has meant a sustained antagonism towards the primary terms in which
pupils conceive the world and themselves in it. Instead of
encouraging pupils to articulate their image of the world
so that it could be developed into something stronger, wider,

more pliable by contact with some of its deeper sources, traditional schooling demanded the suppression of their current image of the world and its summary replacement by an approved version.

The error here was not that one form of culture was effectively upheld at the expense of another (for pupils still *experienced* the world in terms of their own images) but that, failing to acknowledge and accommodate contemporary culture as realized in the consciousness of living individuals, schooling failed to convey meaningfully the additional cultural resources in which it specialized. It neglected the *relationship* between current and enshrined elements of the same culture, and therefore failed to restore the enshrined elements to real currency.

Even in otherwise enlightened argument we are still liable to find formal education represented as opposed to, rather than more positively related to, ordinary life : 'What appears to be real society is not real society at all, but only the transient appearance of society. The permanent form of human society is the form that can only be studied in the arts and sciences.'[5] But what is the difference between the arts and sciences and the mass media? In essence simply that the arts and sciences have a longer memory and a greater degree of internal consistency. This is made possible by putting a hypothetical boundary around them, protecting them from the too rapid impact of shifting influences and impressions, and so building up a more intense, more thoroughly cross-referenced network of interdependent concepts. But (as we describe more fully in chapter 6) the arts and sciences have always been dependent on the world of shifting impressions for their subject matter, their context, and indeed for the intellectual stimulus that comes from transitory problems needing to be solved. Everything that is now enshrined in the academic canons was originally created to solve a problem in the society of its day; for even the problems addressed in art and history – how to conceive of one's society and oneself, how to decide what value to put upon which aspects of life – are very much problems of ordinary, 'transient' reality. The detachment of the arts and sciences from ordinary society is strictly temporary and provisional.

And of course, there are more vehicles of thought in society than just the mass media or the arts and sciences. Of more fundamental importance than either is ordinary colloquial speech, without which neither could exist. The schools' traditional hostility to popular culture is equalled by their deafness to pupils' talk. But, as we shall presently argue, this posture has as sterile a relation to what it claims to revere as to what it disdains.

It is not that 'the academic disciplines' or 'the arts and sciences' are irrelevant. Whether or not particular areas of knowledge are directly and obviously relevant to today's problems is not the only valid criterion for their inclusion in or exclusion from the school curriculum. What is dormant today may be highly relevant again tomorrow. Or it may be mere superficiality that fails to see just how relevant a thing is. The value of particular areas of knowledge may be more in their deep conceptual structure, which may prove transferable to very different subject matters, than in their overt subject matter. Besides, what one becomes interested in at any time thereby *becomes* relevant.*

Conversely, there can be little enlightenment in a simple adherence to the idea of pupils' self-expression without any interest in the *content* of what they express and the problems inherent in it. These problems will in many respects be the very same as those treated in the arts and sciences; and a true interest in pupils' self-expression will also be an interest in the potential connections between it and formal knowledge. Popular cries for relevance in education can best be understood as appeals for the relationship between formal subjects and contemporary experience to be demonstrated, rather than for an exclusive concentration on glaringly topical subjects.

NOTES

[1] This is among the major findings of N. A. Flanders,

quoted by Harold Rosen (in Barnes, Britton and Rosen, p. 120 – see note 2 below). Other researchers in the 'classroom interaction' tradition following on from Flanders's work have produced comparable findings.

[2] Douglas Barnes, James Britton and Harold Rosen, *Language, the Learner and the School* (Penguin, revised edition, 1971).

[3] See Schools Council/Nuffield Foundation, *The Humanities Project, An Introduction* (London, Heinemann Educational, 1970).

[4] Rosen in Barnes, Britton and Rosen, op. cit., p. 125.

[5] Northrop Frye, 'The definition of a university' in Bruce Rusk (ed.), *Alternatives in Education* (University of London Press, 1972), pp. 50-1.

Chapter 3
The pupils' culture

Schools are often criticized for teaching 'middle class culture'. What exactly this culture might be we comment on in the next chapter. Here we are concerned with the implied alternative – a working class culture. Does it exist?

WORKING CLASS CULTURE

Any cultural element, once current, may circulate in any part of society, and thus is liable to become part of the common culture. But there are undeniably elements in the common culture which originate among working class people and which are only discovered by middle class society later, whether or not they then adopt them. Regional dialect, folklore, folk song, proverb and rhyming slang would be examples; the traditions of trade union solidarity would be another. If such examples do not seem at first sight so glorious as the enshrined culture of high art, that is because enshrined art is only the carefully preserved pinnacle of its genre. The quality and vigour of social life depend just as vitally on the diffuse as on the enshrined culture, possibly more so.

We can never set 'middle class culture' and 'working class

culture' side by side to compare them. As soon as it is known and acknowledged by the middle class, working class culture has become part of common currency. Till then it is half invisible, because it is not centralized. It is often regional, or industry-specific, and therefore does not constitute *a* culture shared by the whole working class. Conversely, the culture of the middle classes is not a unified or evenly-spread culture either. The cultural heritage nurtured in universities and prescribed in schools is hardly common currency among accountants, insurance salesmen and department store managers.

The attempt to list features of authentic working class culture such as brass bands, pigeon-fancying, pubs and football, though it does draw our attention to entire aspects of life which we tend to undervalue or ignore, is faintly absurd, inviting the wrong sorts of conclusion, as if these were the working class answer to Shakespeare, Beethoven and Michelangelo. The image of working class culture concocted to 'answer' official culture suffers from just the same sort of institutionalized reverence which falsely reveres official culture, immobilizing it by seeing it as a static object. Where culture is living, that is to say where it is spontaneously drawn upon as a source of values and reference points for real behaviour and experience, it is in a negotiable, fluid state, continually revalued and remade. Thus working class people may discover or rediscover Shakespeare and Beethoven, and thereby change the cultural significance of these figures, just as middle class people may belatedly discover the charm of music hall or the genius of early film comedy.

We may discern at least five strands in culture: working class as such (e.g. trade unionism); regional; popular (in the mass media sense); middle class commercial; and academic. Now the confrontation in schools is not a confrontation between any of these five strands of culture in a fairly pure form and any other. If it were, it would be a meaningless impersonal process, as abstract as our categories, in which the beliefs, attitudes and experiences of teachers and pupils as living people were incidental. The culture of the school is a synthesis of influences, the academic and middle class influences being strong – but not necessarily swallowed whole or well digested. The culture of the pupils is again a synthesis of influences, regional, working class and popular influences being strong – but not necessarily mature or exclusive. Because culture is something which each person or group recreates for itself there is always a possibility of the addition of original elements. Much may be inherited but nothing is inherited passively. What is not at least endorsed is dead weight and not truly part of the culture. Thus when we criticize schools for rejecting the pupils' culture, what we are criticizing is not, essentially, the rejection of a uniform body of values or attitudes but of the pupils' *autonomous thought*, with all its variations and varied influences.

The place of the mass media and popular culture in the thought of pupils is often singled out as a particular enemy of the 'real' or valuable culture with which the school identifies. There is indeed much to object to in popular culture if by this we mean – as many conservative educationists appear to – all cultural phenomena *directed at*, as well as emanating from, the populace. It has been argued that 'the essence of popular culture lies in its stimulation of a consumer approach to life.'[1] Yet there are important differences between such things as advertising, which is only directed at people and not influenced by them in turn, and such things as pop music, which is modified and changed by the people at whom it is directed.

POP MUSIC

The development of pop music over the last two decades is of particular interest, for in this period its susceptibility to the influence of new performers arising from among its primary audience has visibly increased. This shift has been accompanied by a marked improvement in quality, contradicting the conservative assumption that quality and popularity are by nature antagonistic. Not only are more pop songs musically interesting and original (despite the large number that remain derivative and 'commercial') but the *words* of the best songs have improved beyond recognition, becoming in many cases a vehicle for social comment and poetic sentiment of some depth. Simultaneously the *diversity* of available fare in this genre has multiplied, incorporating influences from Western and Indian classical music, medieval and Renaissance music and modern experimental styles. Also the autonomous activity stimulated by the improvements has been widespread – more people play instruments, more people make their own music.

The development of the verbal element is particularly noteworthy since it undeniably comes from the performers themselves, not from the promoters. This has elicited not the slightest critical recognition from broadcasters, 'commercial' or 'establishment', who studiously avoid any reference to the *content*, musical or verbal, of the songs. The performers' attention to words, which we can assume to be shared by the audience, runs counter to many assumptions about the debasing intellectual tendencies of popular entertainment in general and this genre in particular. It was only when performers such as the Beatles, the Rolling Stones, Bob Dylan, the Kinks, the Who, the Incredible String Band and others gained the scope to be exploratory in both music and words, breaking through the old formulae of predictable love songs, that it became common for the words of songs to be printed on the backs of LP sleeves. Genuine emotional and social expression gradually broke through the hollow formulae, and at times achieved remarkable heights.

Of course, this does not settle by any means the quality of the best and worst of pop music or how it compares with items from the established canon. But this is not very important since the two are not in competition with each other, except in the minds of some educationists. The marked improvement in the quality of pop music over the past decade makes it invalid to relegate 'youth culture' or 'pop culture' to some wholly inferior order from that of 'real' culture. This point is not affected by the fact that a great deal of pop music is still of poor quality (as much 'classical' music which has now disappeared must also have been) nor that the commercial pressures are constantly tend-ing to clash with the striving for quality. It is no longer excusable to fail to distinguish between the *popular* and the *commercial* elements in mass culture, or to fail to see that they are often antagonistic. Commercial pressures will always tend to try and spread the available talent as thin as possible. It is not popular taste but commercial pressures and commercial assumptions about popular taste that are hostile to high quality in art and entertainment.

TEACHING AS CULTURAL SYNTHESIS

In many cases one would want to make out an analogous case for *films*, which have similarly been dismissed *en bloc* by many custodians of establishment culture but have reached even more decisive heights, many of them simultaneously with wide popularity and sometimes against the pressures of commercial interests.[2] Further, the work of a number of writers[3] and producers has shown that television can equally be a medium for high quality creative work, apart from its obvious potential for the dissemination of information.

To think this position through, however, is not to come to the conclusion that school should simply replace its adherence to establishment culture by an adherence to popular culture. There needs to be *acknowledgement of* and *engagement with* the pupils' autonomous thought and tastes but there is no point in school simply becoming an additional channel for artefacts which are already current in the informal culture. On the contrary, it must seek ways to complement the informal culture, both by accelerating the development of critical faculties, by giving time, opportunity and help for the deeper analysis of themes touched on in popular culture, *and* by introducing pupils to parts of the culture which do not circulate informally.

We have said that culture is always re-created, not passively inherited; and teaching is itself a means of participating in the creation of new cultural syntheses. This is one reason why the job makes such great demands on one's creative energies. This function of teaching is not adequately described by saying that the teacher introduces pupils to 'the accepted values' or the 'cultural heritage' of our society, as if the necessary values were laid down in some universally valid teachers' handbook and need only be passed on mechanically. Whether one looks to contemporary popular culture, contemporary 'high' culture, 'the culture of the past' or the 'academic disciplines', one finds only endless diversity of artefacts, values and critical opinions. The synthesis from various sources which is made together by teachers and pupils in the course of their encounter is either part of the creative development of both parties or it is a dead weight.

To be capable of this kind of creativity, a teacher needs to be intellectually self-confident enough not to take refuge in some mythical school culture; not to pretend that he does not live in essentially the same cultural world as his pupils, seeing many of the same television programmes and films, listening to the same music, laughing at the same jokes, even, often, reading the same newspapers. Conversely, he needs to be independent-minded in relation to the further cultural resources which his own higher education has made accessible to him, not pretending they mean more to him than they really do, and not using them as a stick to beat popular culture with, if in his own private life he actually finds the two compatible, and even mutually illuminating.

LANGUAGE

Language is the encompassing medium of all culture, and teachers' attitudes to what their pupils say and how they say it is perhaps the key element in determining whether the classroom encounter is to be fruitful or not. The education of teachers makes little provision for the understanding of the fact that all teaching is the teaching of language, though the colleges of education appear to have made a better start in this area than the university departments.[4]

Without wishing to cast any doubt on the importance of the area which Bernstein[5] has opened up, one is uneasy about the widespread use in educational circles of the terms 'restricted' and 'elaborated codes', simply because they seem to dovetail so neatly with pre-existing prejudices about working class intellectual inferiority.[6] Current ideas on the superiority of middle class language are very much a two-edged sword. They offer a plausible explanation as to why working class children do poorly in our education system; they also suggest what it is that the so-called middle class teacher has to offer the working class pupil now that much of the traditional repertoire of educational subject matter is losing its conviction – his 'superior' language.

At the same time the idea of the restricted code can easily become a *justification* for the failure of the working class child in school, and may form an unselfcritical legitimation of a range of negative teaching expectations.[7] If you 'know' that working class pupils are 'linguistically deprived', you are likely to find evidence of this in anything they may say that you happen to find strange or difficult to understand, including original ideas and reflections of parts of the culture with which you are not familiar. Your 'sympathy' for their 'linguistic inability' may simply be a sophisticated way of not hearing what they have to say.

Similar reservations should be made about the idea of 'cultural deprivation' in general. It is unjustified to speak of material and cultural deprivation in the same breath, as if they were the same sort of thing and were automatically mixed up together. This is equivalent to assuming that if you are materially poor you are also spiritually poor – a conjunction which was once thought to be most unlikely.

It is likely that where parents are harassed in their work situation, where the father does long overtime, where accommodation is crowded, or where there is a lack of nourishing food, the disadvantages will affect many aspects of life. But it is quite a different order of statement to speak of cultural deprivation. Culture is not a commodity like food and shelter, of which one can be deprived in the sense that one simply does not have enough. Culture is any group of people's shared way of understanding and celebrating life. There is not a limited supply of this, which can be withheld by the powerful, nor is there any reason to think that the thoughts of poorer people are inferior to those of richer. But assumptions to this effect would be likely to reinforce any tendency the teacher might have to deny the authenticity of working class children's thoughts. And any such tendency would go some way to explain the failure of those children at school, both through discouragement and through non-recognition of their abilities.

If one penalizes the ordinary language habits of children, this will probably be experienced as rejection by the children themselves. Our unwillingness to accept the pupil's self-image as he presents it as a basis for anything further, as we would accept the account of himself given us by a peer, is not due to the failure to apply some particular teaching technique. It is the issue of habitual assumptions about our having nothing much to learn from working class pupils, or perhaps from children and adolescents in general; except, if our curriculum theory is particularly up to date, the exact level of their conceptual incompetence. To put it more simply, we do not encounter pupils very much as human beings. It is rare for teachers to show pupils that they are interested in their out-of-school lives.

A PUPILS' DISCUSSION

Certain assumptions of conventional schooling would, we believe, be exploded by careful and unprejudiced listening to what pupils say about their own concerns: such assumptions as that only 'academic' pupils are capable of abstract thought and interested in philosophical problems. We will include here a transcript of a relatively spontaneous discussion among a class of 'remedial' fourth year leavers (before the raising of the school leaving age) in a secondary modern school. We offer no proof as to the representativeness of this example but the level of discussion was characteristic of the group, and we do not believe that this group was exceptional of its kind. Sometimes they were bored and unresponsive, as conventional schooling would tend to assume them to be all the time.

The discussion, which took place a month before the end of the school year, was begun on the suggestion of one of the boys (Teddy) who simply said as he came into the lesson, 'Let's talk about life after death.' The transcript begins at a point after various anecdotes about ghosts and ouija boards had been recounted. A tape recorder was handy, by chance; the discussion was volatile, and not all of it could be deciphered later. Breaks in continuity are indicated by three dots across the page, but it will be seen that a basic thematic unity prevailed. The transcript is as faithful as possible within reason, but of course much of the tone, emphasis and animation is lost.[8]

Editorial interjections are in brackets.

DAVE: We used to have a laugh, scaring people with masks.

TEACHER: What did you do?

DAVE: Just kept following them, making noises. They didn't half run!

TEDDY: What about the bloke with the bandages round his head then? He put them round his head to frighten people.

TEACHER: When was that?

TEDDY: A long time ago it was. He used to hide round corners and then come out with bandages round his head.

TEACHER: Why were the people frightened?

JIM: How do you mean – bandages?

BRIAN: It's their imagination. They've got a very good imagination.

TEDDY: You know – bandages.

TEACHER: Have we all got the same imagination?

JIM: How do you mean – bandages?

ALL: No.

TEDDY: You know – bandages – wrapped round his head.

JIM: Oh.

(simultaneous)

* * *

TEDDY: I don't know what they're scared of. There's nothing to be sacred of – they (spirits) can't hurt you if they're dead.

JIM: There are poltergeists.

TEACHER: If they don't harm you, why are people frightened?

TEDDY: That's a load of (raspberry noise) 'cause if you see one, right, you're not going to just stand there, saying they can't hurt me, are you? You're going to faint or something like that and when you wake up you're going to be hysterical. You'll probably lose your mind.

* * *

GRAHAM: They don't believe in them because they haven't seen them.

MARY: I heard that when you look at them they take away your eyesight.

TEACHER: Why?

MARY: So that you can't see them any more.

TEDDY: I believe in God, right, but I haven't seen him. Look at all the people who believe in God and haven't seen him.

JIM: When we were at school camp we were all frightened – we hung hangers on the back of the door.

GRAHAM: You can't prove there's been a World War if you haven't seen it.

DAVE: Oh shut up. There are people alive who have been there.

TEACHER: How do we know there are desks in this room?

BRIAN: Because there's things on it.

GRAHAM: Because you can see them.

TEDDY: It might be your imagination.

JIM: (sitting on desk) Well if it is, I'll fall through it.

TEDDY: It might be your imagination. Say Mr Jones walked in that door there, walked out of that door and then came in that door again. What would happen then?

CLIVE: He must have had a quick walk round!

TEDDY: It's your imagination isn't it?

TEACHER: Could I be imagining that all you are in here?

ALL: Yes.

GRAHAM: If you put your mind to it you can.

* * *

TEACHER: (after someone mentioned dreams) What about dreams – can they tell you anything?

TEDDY: Yes. This is true. You can ask Mr Smith or Stuart. I said I had a dream I was going to get kicked in the face in games. As soon as I got on the pitch I got kicked in the face and my nose started bleeding.

* * *

TEDDY: Well, Hitler – they haven't found his body yet, have they? Well, what happened to it?

BRIAN: Perhaps he didn't really exist.

JIM: We've got films of him though.

GRAHAM: They could have been man-made.

JIM: They couldn't. You're going on about ghosts and things but this isn't the same thing. These are real things.

TEDDY: They say photographers can fix films, right? Well, what about that then? He might not have ...

GRAHAM: What about the Olympic Games in Munich?

JIM: What about it? Oh look, we know he was real, we just know it.

TEDDY: You say if you see a ghost you know it ain't real. Look if you saw a ghost – what would happen? If you saw a spirit or ghost what would you say?

JIM: I'd say it ain't real.

TEDDY: Yeah, what would happen then? It wouldn't go away like that.

JIM: How do you know?

GRAHAM: You'd run like hell.

JIM: It might be my imagination.

TEDDY: You wouldn't have the guts to say that.

JIM: It couldn't be real – I know that myself.

TEACHER: If you don't believe in them, would you ever see one?

JIM: No, I don't think so.

* * *

TEACHER: What might people be frightened of if they're not frightened of spirits?

CLIVE: Everything else in the dark.

DAVE: Your imagination.

JIM: I'd still be scared though, even though I don't believe in them.

GRAHAM: Things stay in your mind.

CLIVE: You can't get it out till morning. Light sort of wears it away.

*   *   *

TEDDY: Why do we have dreams?

TEACHER: Dave had a book about dreams. Dave, did it say anything about why people have them?

DAVE: It said about the meanings of them. But it didn't make sense to me.

*   *   *

TEDDY: I cut myself once. I fell over in a lot of grass and didn't know it was bleeding. I thought it was alright and walked down the road and got indoors and when I took my clothes off, it was all blood.

GRAHAM: I put my foot through a caravan window. I put it straight through and I never had no cut on me at all ...

JIM: I thought I'd just bruised my hand but I'd fractured it ...

GRAHAM: Then when I came home from holiday there was this scar there ...

JIM: You can't feel it though.

GRAHAM: It could have been there before.

BRIAN: It's mind over matter.

TEACHER: What does that mean?

TEDDY: Mind's stronger than body.

TEACHER: Is mind stronger than body?

BRIAN: Yes, it must be.

TEDDY: If your mind controls your body, it must be.

*   *   *

GRAHAM: Whenever I go in a church I always feel frightened. I never feel safe in churches.

JIM: You know St Mary's church. I was told that if you run round about twenty times on the stroke of midnight before one second is over, you'd never die.

BRIAN: There are two coffins there and people say that they had the Black Death. The tops of the tombs have been pushed open and they say that if you run round there twelve times at midnight – it's possibly mind over matter—you'll see the whole thing completely open.

* * *

GRAHAM: There's a lady who thinks she's James II.

TEACHER: Dave, what is this about reincarnation that you mentioned before?

DAVE: You come back as another being.

TEACHER: Does this mean that we've all been here before?

DAVE: Yeah, that's what my old dear reckons.

BRIAN: You'd probably remember if you'd been here before.

TEDDY: I heard you die and then come back as an animal. We were apes, right? Maybe the apes turn into like us.

JIM: How do we know? 'Cause they're dying and they might be coming back.

TEDDY: In the Bible it says that Christ made us and put us on the earth. How did he put us on – just like this or like apes? It's been proved that it was apes.

JIM: Who was supposed to be the first on? Adam and Eve? What can we believe?

TEDDY: Yeah, but how do you get Chinese people, you know all different languages and coloured people?

TEACHER: I think Genesis is a story – a way of explaining life.

GRAHAM: There could have been another earth, a century before this or after.

BRIAN: Did you know there is such a thing as a time barrier?

TEACHER: What does that mean?

BRIAN: You can go forward in time.

TEDDY: Or backward. What about that bloke who said there was going to be a war?

TEACHER: H. G. Wells?

TEDDY: Yeah, he said there was going to be a First World War and a Second World War. And he said man was going to go on the moon. He could see into the future.

CLIVE: He must have guessed, hoping he was right.

TEDDY: *Guessed?*

GRAHAM: He never named the date when man would land on the moon. Hundreds of years ago they said man would land on the moon.

CLIVE: They might have known man could do it.

TEDDY: How? *How?*

CLIVE: I don't know how.

TEDDY: Well then.

TEACHER: A long time ago a man called Leonardo da Vinci was devising ways in which man could fly.

BRIAN: Two people have flown. One died—one went too near the sun and burnt the wings.

TEACHER: That's a story – it's about Icarus.

BRIAN: But it could be true.

GRAHAM: They said once that you could never have planes made out of heavy metal.

BRIAN: They say that to fly you would have to have a chest about six feet long.

GRAHAM: We're getting too crowded so we've got to move further and further ...

JIM: Everybody says we shouldn't fly because we haven't got wings and we shouldn't swim because ...

BRIAN: ... we haven't got gills.

JIM: But we'd be stuck here all the time.

GRAHAM: The earth is getting more crowded and people want to get further away from the earth and find other things.

TEDDY: Why do people die? Why can't they live on for ever and ever?

GRAHAM: People in Victorian times only used to live up to forty or thirty years old and people are living over a hundred now. Food's getting better.

TEDDY: I'll tell you why, when women had children the wife or the baby used to die. Yeah, but if they're trying to cut down on babies why are they giving these new drugs and ladies having seven or eight babies?

It would be a superficial reaction to regard this conversation as simply so much gossip. The pupils keep returning from different angles to certain underlying themes of great seriousness: appearance and reality, the supernatural, fear, death, prediction of events, the power of the mind. The images and instances are not purely accidental associations but are brought up as examples to test abstract propositions. The capacity of the group to sustain a dialogue on these themes over a long period – about an hour – and despite periods of confusion when several people were talking together (mostly left out) is evidence of a high level of interest and conceptualization. Yet these pupils were conspicuous failures by conventional school standards. Their last school marks – a mock CSE exam – ranged from 3 to 16 per cent. This was because their reading and writing were poor. But there would be no other official judgement on their entire mental capabilities. When the transcript was brought back to the class to read together, two other pupils had to take the parts of Teddy and Graham – they could not read. Yet Teddy was perhaps the most articulate of all, continually raising pertinent questions and introducing examples that furthered the investigation.

The main themes preoccupying the group could not have been more relevant to the basic concerns of science, history, religion and social affairs. Yet to judge by the feeling of a lack of stable reference points and a lack of ways of substantiating their ideas, school had not enabled these pupils to make connections between their own preoccupations and the relevant areas of formal knowledge. Interest and conceptual ability – the things that are usually said to be missing – are present in abundance; but what a school could provide – secure reference points and techniques of structuring inquiry – are missing. So also is the confidence which would be needed to listen patiently and respond less defensively. These were pupils who were choosing to leave school at the earliest opportunity. Clearly school had not made them aware of what it had to offer.

It is important to recognize that, despite the apparent

background role taken by the teacher, this dialogue might very well not have taken place outside school conditions. School provided firstly a time and place; secondly, an adult who could ensure that no one person monopolised the discussion, and who, by taking the pupils seriously, helped them to take themselves seriously. Also, the teacher's questions, though not always entirely apt, are accepted as stimulants and enlarge the scope of the discussion. Although there is no attempt to direct the discussion, the questions have the function of helping pupils to focus on some of the more crucial issues raised, such as subjectivity. This does not mean that the teacher's questions were other than spontaneous reactions to what was being discussed – except that they were carefully open-ended and tentative. Teachers who have been used to the notion of themselves as sources of authoritative knowledge may feel that the new value put upon pupils' talk and ideas threatens to make them redundant. This is not at all the case.

We are not suggesting that all lessons should be like this but that a fair proportion should be. A good discussion is not always possible, and opportunities should be taken when they arise. Apart from the value to the pupils in terms of developing articulateness, learning from each other, building up confidence in relationship and reasoning power, such lessons provide the teacher with invaluable information on the interests and conceptual needs of the group of pupils. After a lesson spent like this the teacher would be able to select material for a more structured lesson and tailor its presentation much more closely to the group, with a greater chance of its 'taking'. Without attempting to disprove or inhibit points of view that had been expressed, the teacher would present material calculated to extend the conceptual tools available. From this discussion, for example, one could immediately note that the pupils needed ways of handling relative time-spans and of comparing the relative objectivity of various kinds of evidence.

NOTES

[1] G. H. Bantock, *Culture, Industrialization and Education* (London, Routledge and Kegan Paul, 1968), p. 64.

[2] *My Autobiography* by Charles Chaplin (Penguin, 1966; first published by the Bodley Head, 1964) describes some of the conflicts between artistic and commercial interests in the film industry of the thirties and forties.

[3] See for example the plays of David Mercer, whose reputation was first made as a TV writer. Some of his TV plays have been published, e.g. *The Parachute, Let's Murder Vivaldi* and *In Two Minds* (London, Calder and Boyars, 1967).

[4] See David Scarbrough, *Language Study and Teacher Training* (Themes in Education No. 32, University of Exeter Institute of Education, 1973).

[5] See Basil Bernstein, *Class, Codes and Controls. Volume 1, Theoretical Studies Towards a Sociology of Language* (London, Routledge and Kegan Paul, 1973).

[6] A criticism of this aspect of Bernstein's work is made by Harold Rosen in *Language and Class, A Critical Look at the Theories of Basil Bernstein* (Bristol, Falling Wall Press, 1972).

[7] An account of the 'teacher expectation' literature will be found in Douglas A. Pidgeon, *Expectation and Pupil Performance* (Slough, National Foundation for Educational Research, 1970).

[8] We would like to thank the pupils whose discussion this is. A shortened version of this transcript appeared in *Rank and File* 21/*Blackbored* 5 (undated, issued autumn 1972) under the title 'Light sort of wears it away'; and in *Language and Class Workshop* 1 (London, Language and Class Group, 1974).

Chapter 4

Middle class culture

We have argued that schools tend to reject pupils' culture, even though this culture is one largely shared by the teachers in their private lives. The question now is: in favour of what does this rejection take place?

The usual indictment is that schools purvey 'middle class culture'. The middle class, in any interpretation would include a wide range of occupations, from shop managers, brokers, accountants, lawyers and small businessmen to lecturers, doctors, broadcasters and Members of Parliament. Whatever these groups may share in the way of values – possibly a high valuation of individual achievement, possibly more questionable traits such as a tendency to derogate working class achievements – there must clearly be a great deal of diversity in their lifestyles and values. One of the things that would not be found equally among them is an attachment to 'high' culture, the version of culture on which the social and intellectual aims of traditional schooling are said to be based.

However, it is most unlikely that one would be able to trace much connection between the scores of statements made every day by teachers to pupils, whether in particular lessons or in the school generally, and values which might reasonably be attributed to 'high culture' rather than any other source. Schools tend to highlight (verbally) any more or less 'decent' attitudes – respectability, responsibility, hard work, charitable feelings and so on. Among these one would certainly find an emphasis on competitiveness, reinforced through the selective structures of the school itself. But if the effect of this is to elicit respect for 'middle class values', it is a respect from the outside, for it is not the aim of the middle class, or of the school on its behalf, to recruit the mass of pupils into its own ranks.

A PHANTOM CULTURE

In progressive and egalitarian criticisms of the education system there is a certain amount of confusion between the criticism of schools as teaching middle class values and as simply failing to teach effectively.[1] Thus we are scandalized by the fact that working class pupils are at a drastic disadvantage in our schools, yet this disadvantage is chiefly known by the fact that the pupils are not successful according to the schools' criteria – which, however, we also in part reject. Working class pupils score lower on tests of 'ability and attainment' which are geared to what the education system considers to be worthwhile knowledge and skills. If we are unhappy with this state of affairs, does this mean that the greater success of working class pupils as measured by these same norms would be a highly desirable thing, and would it answer the case?

The answer is surely that it would be a desirable thing but not in itself sufficient. Our legitimate criticism of schools is a compound of two distinct criticisms, the first a criticism of what school does to those who fail in it and the second of what it does to those who succeed.

Education seeks to develop knowledge, techniques and values. Knowledge and techniques (skill in mathematics, art, science, music, language, sport, etc.) are not value-free in the sense that they can ever be detached from values, but they are *value-transferable* : they can be employed in the service of varied, even contradictory, values. To teach them well is to teach their principles, and thus to teach them *as* transferable.

There is a fundamental dilemma within progressive thought as to how far cultural and technical resources developed in hierarchical societies can be and need to be taken over into an egalitarian society, and how far their absorption would actually impede the development of such a society because they embody social assumptions hostile to it. The problem is simply not grasped in injunctions to 'put an end to capitalism' or 'smash the system' since at the same time 'the system' is interpreted as ubiquitous and all-pervasive; in these terms it is impossible to distinguish what must be interpreted as intrinsic to the system and what as belonging to forces opposing it from within – which is presumably the only place it can be opposed from if it is ubiquitous. This dilemma ought to put firmly onto the agenda of egalitarians today the problem of how much and what kind of continuity is inevitable or desirable between the present and *any* immediately superseding form of society. To say 'none' is to say nothing in the guise of saying everything.[2]

The most glaring fault of schools is not their successful inculcation of undesirable values but their failure to convey to most pupils even the questionable skills and knowledge which they say they are trying to convey.

We can distinguish at least four separate channels by which values are conveyed in the school: (a) actual constraints – rules and punishments; (b) value statements made by teachers in their own right or on behalf of the school; (c) value statements attributed by the teacher to the subject matter but actually deriving from contemporary social norms or the norms of the school or the teacher (e.g. using Shakespeare to authenticate present-day patriotism; using the failure of revolutions as a warning against rebelliousness; using scientific objectivity to disqualify personal conviction); (d) values more genuinely embodied in the subject matter and successfully made accessible by the teacher.

Of these four kinds of value, the fourth, the genuine contact with subject matter, is probably heavily overwhelmed by the other three kinds as far as most of the school population is concerned. Except for pupils in grammar schools and the top streams in comprehensives (between them a small minority of the total school population) secondary school experience is largely made up of the other three kinds of message. If they are objectionable it is because they often amount to an insistence on subordination and an attack on autonomous thought. This is not adequately described by calling it the inculcation of middle class values. The operation is essentially a negative one – one in which values, along with curiosity, confidence and autonomy, are lost rather than gained.

For the successful pupils the case is different. Here there is probably a successful amplification of values, and some of these values – personal success at all costs, stress on individual rather than social goals, absorption of human criteria into commercial ones – might validly be described as middle class. But by no means all the values passed on, implicitly or explicitly, by the school to the successful minority of pupils could be put in this category. Teachers do not pass on a canon of values prescribed for them by 'the system' but the content of their own particular compromises with that system – and their own struggles within it. English teachers frequently see themselves as purveying anti-commercial criteria, history teachers as purveying values of social responsibility, science teachers as inculcating values of independent critical thinking. Of these kinds of values we could hardly say that they were undesirable.

Thus the improvements we seek in education are firstly a revaluation of subject matter and techniques, and secondly the making of the revalued material accessible to all pupils. But for the more immediate aims the priority is likely to be reversed : primarily to overcome the inefficiency of education and its self-defeating preoccupation with squashing the autonomous thought processes of pupils; and, aided by this, a revaluation of the skills and subject matters. What is wrong with the schools is not that they do not teach egalitarian values but that they do not *embody* the primary value of equal benefits to all pupils. Without this, even the most progressive subject matter would be frustrated; with it, egalitarian values become meaningful.

The middle class values that are conveyed to the successful minority of pupils cannot, in so far as they are undesirable, simply be equated with the 'cultural heritage', though they are bound up with mystifying, reverent but actually rather detached attitudes *towards* that heritage.[3] The 'academic canons' are not intrinsically either good or bad. There are both desirable and undesirable values to be found expressed in literature, history and all subjects that embody values. There are other subjects, not only the pure sciences but physical education and drawing, for example, which embody valuable and value-transferable techniques, even though the teaching of these techniques is rarely free from value statements and assumptions (such as competitiveness – but also team spirit – in sport, reverence for – or genuine appreciation of – art, and independence of social responsibility – or true open-mindedness – in science). It is important to maintain a distinction between values attributed to subject matter by teachers and values embodied in subject matter, which may be easily seen in history, religion, social studies and so on. The difference is not absolute – any subject matter is still influenced, in classroom presentation, by the teacher's selection and emphasis; but values genuinely embodied in subject matter have a chance of transcending this framework once the pupil discovers that he has *direct* access to them and that they may go far beyond, or even contradict, the teacher's presentation.

Where school rules and punishments are extensive and anti-educational, there is little opportunity for values of any kind, desirable or not, to be genuinely internalized by pupils. The only value that is conveyed is the strongly implicit one of the desirability and correctness of subordination – but it is doubtful whether this is truly *learnt* by pupils or merely encountered as a feature of this particular environment which must be negotiated.

Where pure control is slightly less of a preoccupation, the value statements made by teachers in their own persona have more chance of carrying over (for example the value of loyalty to institutions implied in doing things 'for the name of the school'). Where the value statements made by the teachers in their own right do carry over, there is a possibility of values also being successfully carried over by association with certain subject matters. And only where all these previous kinds of value are digestible by pupils is there a likelihood of values or subject content being successfully brought out.

On the whole it is the lower orders of value statement that present the far more urgent problem. It is not that undesirable values embodied in traditional subject matter are effectively taught, but that values at a much lower level, of control and subordination, are so prevalent as virtually to exclude the successful conveying of values either good or bad that genuinely have their source in the cultural heritage. To be more precise, if one divides education roughly according to class lines, having in mind on the one hand, say the 15 per cent or so of pupils who go on to higher education and on the other hand the 85 per cent who do not, the nature of the crisis of education for these two groups is different. For the 85 per cent, the complaint is that there is little genuine education taking place; for the 15 per cent, the problems lie in the nature of the values successfully conveyed.

Of these two kinds of complaint, clearly the complaints that might be made on behalf of the 15 per cent would be subtler than those of the 85 per cent. This does not mean they are unimportant, since these 15 per cent then go on to be more influential in society (at least superficially) than the 85 per cent, and so the values which they have absorbed become more widely diffused. For example, teachers themselves come into this category, and the value statements that they make directly to pupils without references to any subject matter are nevertheless probably influenced to some degree by their own higher education. (Yet it is still very much an open question to what extent higher education itself conveys judgements which are not actually derived from the subject matter of the disciplines.)

When one considers the prevalence in schools of state-

ments by teachers like : 'Stop it', 'Be quiet when I'm talking',
'I'm not interested in what you think', 'Don't speak until
you're spoken to'; sarcastic comments of varying degrees of
wit; statements which gratuitously induce a poor self-image
in the students, such as 'Now listen, thickies!', 'You lot
wouldn't be any good at this', 'Why do they always give
me the worst classes?', 'Those are my bright ones over there.
The dull ones are over here' (said to a visitor in the hearing
of the class); offensive statements based on inexplicit value
judgements, like 'They didn't teach you much out there, did
they?', 'When are you going to learn to fit in with our way
of life?' (to coloured children); or, as one head said in an
assembly 'Now I'm going to say this simply, so that everyone can understand it, even 1X' (1X being a bottom stream
form) – when one considers the prevalence of these kinds of
statement, the questionable content of actual subject matters
seems a relatively mild offence.

However, the two types of offence no doubt reinforce one
another. It seems likely that where there is a strong substitution of control for teaching there would also be a predom-
inance of subject matters ill chosen for the particular pupils
(since there is no respect for or interest in the pupils' existing state of mind); and that the values which *are* successfully
brought out in the subject matter are not likely to be values
conducive to independent thought or social criticism, since
these attributes are clearly not valued by the teachers.

All the statements concerned essentially with the relationship between the school and the pupils, and with control,
do themselves amount to a huge overall value 'statement',
namely the desirability of subordination and the correctness
of relinquishing initiative. It seems most unlikely that any
teacher would bother to try and authenticate this value
'statement' by reference to the subject matter of the disciplines (though it could, with certain contortions, be done).
But it does have a direct connection, in the school experience,
with that *dis*qualification of the pupil's autonomous values
and culture which is treated as being necessary to the right
valuing of the 'heritage'. The implicit rationale of all the
controlling activity is that it is necessary in order to permit

learning to take place, yet it is not noticed that beyond a certain level, and because there is no attempt to gain the internalized consent of pupils for what rules may be gen-uninely necessary, the controlling activity actually prevents learning from taking place. What we have to grasp about the bad school situations (and they are probably very common) is that the autonomous culture and self-image of the pupils is attacked in the name of values which, however, are not themselves effectively conveyed.

In parts of the 'cultural canon' itself there *are* values that might be thought objectionable. For example, one could find plenty of examples of the glorification of war; and plenty of others which 'teach' that material misery is 'one's own fault'; that collective social action is always ugly and destructive; that women should always be subservient to men, or can only find fulfilment by providing the emotional support for men's achievements; and so on. But one could equally, if with some probing, find the contrary values. Thus it would be false to say or imply that anything authenticated by inclusion in the cultural canon is either necessarily to be admired for its values or, on the other hand, necessarily of value only to a minority ruling class.

Thus in a bad school situation the following features could easily combine: (a) disqualification of pupils' autonomous culture, independent judgement and own experience; (b) sarcasm, contempt, discouragement, etc.; (c) presentation of the heritage as uniformly 'good', to be admired and beyond criticism or controversy. Further illumination of this damaging combination may be gained by looking closely at the last component, the one that superficially seems most positive, and that directly informs the teaching of the 'successful' minority of pupils.

'THE CULTURAL HERITAGE'

A misguided respect for an abstract idealization called 'the cultural heritage' may have the effect of justifying regarding the living culture of contemporary human beings, in all its raggedness and volatility, as wholly degenerate. This dislocated attitude actually represents as great an alienation from the real content of the cultural heritage as from contemporary culture. Genuine respect for the achievements of past culture, with an awareness of how innovatory and controversial they were in their own time, could not but lead to at least a respectful fascination with that part of the culture which is now in the process of formation, and in which we are all involved.

The cultural heritage is an abstraction from the same culture which, however indirectly, furnishes the 'native' (informal) culture of today's pupils out of school. There is a continuum between the two. If the school says, in essence, 'What we are presenting to you is *culture*—something totally different from the values and ideas you live by in the course of your everyday life', it is making it extremely difficult for the pupil to see what is being offered as a potential addition to his personal store of behaviour models, criteria of judgement and reference points of meaning.

Yet this is just how it is presented, for it has lost its inner meaning for many teachers themselves. The reactionary teacher uses 'the established content' of the academic canons to authenticate his own authority. The culture to which he introduces the pupils, is, as far as the classroom transaction is concerned, his 'property'. He enlists Shakespeare, the battle of Waterloo, the parliamentary system to lend credence to whatever values he chooses to purvey; and if this is done at the cost of some internal contradictions between the subject matter and his use of it, these will appear to most pupils as stemming from their own confusion.

In conventional education we find a predominant image of the past as static, either because it is 'finished', as in the presentation of history, or because it is 'eternal', as in the presentation of literature and art. We do not find much attempt to understand the past as it was experienced at the time – that is, as being full of doubt, dispute and danger, as the present is to us. We find little recognition of the fact that our awareness of the past is our vicarious experience of other people's present.

DEAD CULTURE OR DORMANT CULTURE?

At its advent, universal education became the main disseminator of a culture which had till then been firmly in the custody of the powerful and privileged. But only half the actual content of the arts and sciences consists of the accumulated testament of social conservatism and hierarchy; the other half consists of the expropriated record of revolutionary and innovatory ideas over the centuries. The *post facto* appropriation of all art and science – even, or especially, the work of dissenters and radical innovators – by the ruling powers imposes a falsely conservative gloss on these works. There are progressive resources in 'the cultural heritage' which should be rescued by revaluation and made widely accessible. The culture of the past sometimes represents the obverse side to the *power* of the past – its misgivings, its consolations, its trials.

More than that, it would be foolish to see in 'the cultural heritage' only its subject matter and not its qualities as organized thought. This reduction to subject matter has precisely been one of the ways in which traditional education has emasculated the heritage which it purports to disseminate. The important thing for us about Shakespeare is not his patriotism but the degree of integration in his vision of all the features of his society. The patriotism is dated. The concern with social cohesion illuminates even radically different forms of society.

It is precisely when old ideas have lost their grip as dogmas that they become accessible and interesting as optional variations on the human spirit. The modern anthropologist or artist is capable of deriving wisdom and enrichment from primitive myths and taboos because there is no question of his being socially bound by them in the way that their original practitioners were. We ought now to take an anthropological attitude towards the culture of our own past. The resources it yields will be all the richer, the more

aware we are that it can have no authoritative grip upon us
– that we are responsible for creating our own cultural synthesis to answer to the needs of our own chosen form of
society. This gives us a chance to relate to history afresh – to
find its dormant meanings, to discover how far the literary
and philosophic tradition, even before the Romantics, is a
tradition of social criticism, not merely a symposium of
glorification of its patrons; to discover the 'subconscious' of
the past – how it must have looked from the non-ruling class
vantage-point.

This revaluation of the cultural heritage is now going on,
and its insights still have to contend with adherents of the
old schools of shallow culture-worship. The formal education
system, with its inherent conservatism, with its senior teachers still drawing on a higher education received several
decades ago, is the last sector of society to reflect cultural
revaluation. But for the majority of teachers the 'cultural
heritage' has neither the old authority nor yet the new
interest.

The majority of teachers are too bewildered to structure
the new opportunity for revaluation for themselves. They
adhere without conviction to subject matters of which the
use is no longer evident; or, with 'non-academic' pupils, they
thankfully abandon all attempt at cultural prescription and
espouse instead the 'self-expression' and 'discovery' methods
of progressive education, without pretence of criteria for
assessing standards of meaning and achievement in what is
discovered or expressed.

Yet for teachers who can participate in cultural revaluation the cultural heritage acquires new meaning and offers
a multitude of avenues for exploration *with* pupils. For in
the process of revaluation, any relations that can be found
or forged with the pupils' own culture are welcome tools.

THE PAST AS IT WAS WHEN IT WAS THE PRESENT

We would do right to be sceptical of any simplistic con-
traction of the past into a claustrophobic pre-echo of the
present. The historian rightly wants us to appreciate the

'differentness' of the past, not merely the points of similarity with our own times. But the way to achieve this is precisely by relating it to the present – the opposite of confusing it with the present – now in comparison, now in contrast. The appreciation of difference is precisely what is sacrificed by any attempt to use the past to justify the present.

No one, of course, genuinely teaches 'the values of the past' or any such thing in a raw state. Our selection from the accumulated canons is always mediated through contemporary concepts and judgements. The direct encounter with literature is the nearest we can get to a true dialogue with the past, but even the teaching of literature consists only partly (and probably not enough) of direct encounter with literature. The surrounding concepts – the questions asked and answers required – amount to the teaching, in however diluted a form, of modern literary criticism.

This is inevitable. Literary criticism is the store of judgements which form a framework for the valuing of literature. Similarly, the teaching of history is the teaching of modern historical concepts, without which history 'itself' – events, processes, people – would hardly be accessible.

But if it is right and necessary to be teaching through contemporary perspectives, it is equally necessary to make clear to oneself and one's pupils that this is what is being done—that we are looking at the past through the present. But what exactly is the relation of literary criticism to literature or of history the academic discipline to history the subject matter? Simply that the basic content – the work of literature, the historical event – is prior to and greater than the discipline, even though it is the discipline which helps to preserve the work of literature and awareness of the historical event. The discipline consists essentially of *commentary on* the fundamental subject matter. But this cannot have meaning for a pupil until the fundamental subject matter has somehow been made accessible in a more direct form. The point is not that one disputes Shakespeare's achievement but that if one wishes to convey the content of that achievement as distinct from wishing to convey the historical fact that it has been considered great, one has to reproduce the conditions in which that achievement can be appreciated – that is, one has to make his qualities accessible as an experience, not as a piece of knowledge. It is only after this that discussion of the dramatic skills that made the experience possible can have meaning.

Correspondingly, the way to make history meaningful is to make it accessible as an experience. This can only be through initial analogies with contemporary politics or with situations to which the pupils already have some access (e.g. their parents' and relatives' memories), or by raising questions about the origins of social structures or institutions to which the pupils already attach some meaning (e.g. factory life, civil laws, transport).

This is not a mere concession to ignorance. Contemporary experience is an indispensable reference point at both 'ends' of education – both as a means of access to the past and as the revealed meaning of the past. There is a sense in which the working class pupil knows more about the industrial revolution than the history teacher ever will. In saying so, we are merely reiterating that society outside the school is the context in which the value of formal education is ultimately to be judged. We must equally reiterate that this does not mean a capitulation to the values of outside society – impossible in any case since the outside values are themselves in conflict – but a critical engagement with them.

Progressive education today frequently makes the acknowledgement we are asking for – the acknowledgement of the pupil's native culture – but reserves this treatment for those whom it regards as incapable of the 'academic' education which it reserves for the 'more able' pupils. The *continuum* between contemporary culture and the cultural heritage is still unexplored. The very division of pupils into 'academic' and 'non-academic' perpetuates not only self-fulfilling assumptions about most pupils' mental capacities but self-defeating assumptions about the nature of the academic heritage.

If the relationship between the contemporary and the enshrined cultures is denied, if the continuum between them cannot be seen, if all worthwhile criteria are claimed to be embodied exclusively in the enshrined canon, while the neutral title 'art' is denied to films, pop songs and television plays, then the grounding for any internalization of the deeper or extended criteria has been cut away.

The best progressive teaching does not stop short at a mere acknowledgement of the pupils' current culture (including their creative writing, acting and discovering) but seeks to identify the linking stages on the continuum between these and the extended criteria which are thought valuable. The first step in the attempt to internalize extended cultural criteria is to get the pupils to recognize that they already have some critical criteria : that they prefer some films, plays, comics, jokes, books to others, and that this preference has something to do not only with their own moods but also with objective qualities in the preferred artefacts.

THE PRESENT AS THE MEANING OF THE PAST

Psychologically, access to events and ideas which in their own time were contentious and controversial is gained only by analogy with those things which are controversial to *us*. But the relationship of past controversies to present is greater than a merely psychological one (though that alone has profound implications for teaching methods). We can only regard a certain political or cultural issue of the past as 'settled' (and therefore, in conventional academic regard, amenable to objective appraisal) in the sense that history has taken a certain course of development and not another. Now clearly what academics have in mind when they speak of the cultural heritage are the antecedents of our own society. Thus the contentious issues of past days are only settled in the sense that the present-day world is their outcome. But if there is still controversy, as of course there is, about the present features and future destiny of society, historical conflicts leading to the present social condition are themselves *still at issue*. If, as T. S. Eliot said in his essay on Milton, the civil war of the seventeenth century is in a sense still going on, the same can be said of many other of the key conflicts of our history. It is the end of a story which tells us the ultimate significance of what happens in the middle. But we will always be in the middle of the story of our society, and thus judgement of the significance and value of what has already happened is inseparable from judgement of the present, and of the feasibility and desir-ability of possible futures. Cultural and historical judge-ments cannot be justified by reference to 'the past' alone, since the particular picture of the past which is invoked is the one selected by these very judgements.

It is true that in some respects you can only judge the value of a work of art or historical event at some distance from it in time. Yet of course the thing itself occurred or was created for its own time. The motivation of its origin-ators or participants was the solution, or imaginative appre-hension, of the preoccupying problems of its own immediate society. One will see different patterns and aspects 50, 100 or 200 years later but these do not amount to 'objectivity' so much as to the accumulated layers of meaning acquired by the event or artefact with the further development of the issues originally affected or represented. One does not ever therefore come to a final authoritative judgement.

The school's exclusion and censure of contemporary cul-ture is paralleled by its 'freezing' of past culture. The prob-lem of the two levels of schooling (broadly that of the so-called 'academic' and 'non-academic' pupils) is a combined one of *engaging* with contemporary culture and *revaluing* past culture. It would make no sense to oppose the *real* content of past culture as a whole to the pupils' informal culture or to present culture in general; nor, as happens in some progressive classrooms, to recognize the pupils' culture and abandon the traditional one. The main error is the combina-tion of a condemnatory attitude to the pupils' culture and an uncritically reverent, immobilizing one towards the 'heri-tage'. This twin feature of misguided schooling does as great a disservice to what it reveres as to what it denigrates.

EDUCATION AS INTERVENTION, NOT INITIATION

Unfortunately, it is just this combination which is blessed by some of the 'educational philosophy' most widely drawn on in the colleges. It is worth looking closely at an example of this doctrine. In chapter 6 we state more positively what in our view the value of the disciplines and their optimum use in school is.

In R. S. Peters's essay 'Education as initiation'[4] one finds a rapid and uncritical transition from 'mind' as a product of social development to 'mind' as the exclusive property of the academic disciplines. The child

> learns to name objects, to locate his experience in a spatio-temporal framework, and to impose causal and means-to-end categories to make sense of events or actions. ... Such an embryonic mind is the produce of initiation into public traditions enshrined in a public language, which it took our remote ancestors centuries to develop.

This happens, of course (and we don't think Peters at this stage intends otherwise), outside formal education. It happens in the family and immediate early environment. Yet already in this description the image is forming of a static inheritance – 'enshrined' in a language which it took our 'remote ancestors' centuries to develop. The public language – ordinary colloquial discourse – is not seen as being in a state of development *now*; still less is there any hint that the 'embryonic' mind is actually participating in the development of its own language. There is no recognition of the point made strongly by linguists in recent decades – that the acquisition of language (ordinary, colloquial language) is the most complex intellectual and creative achievement that we make in the course of our lives.

But the next few sentences in Peters's 'thumbnail sketch of the social history of mind' are much bolder:

> With the mastery of basic skills the door is open to a vaster and more variegated inheritance. Further differentiation develops as the boy [sic] becomes initiated more deeply into the distinctive forms of knowledge such as

science, history, mathematics, religious and aesthetic appreciation, and into the practical types of knowledge involved in moral, prudential and technical forms of thought and action. Such differentiations are alien to the mind of a child and primitive man – indeed to that of pre-seventeenth-century man. To have a mind ... is to have an awareness differentiated in accordance with the canons implicit in all these inherited traditions.

There are some extraordinary implications here. We are virtually asked to believe that people before the seventeenth century did not have minds worth speaking of; and, by implication, nor did anyone who lived or lives in a culture which does not differentiate 'forms of knowledge' into science, history mathematics, etc., where science, history and mathematics are clearly understood as that version of them now current in Western technological society (the 'implicit canons'). Since all these millions and their entire civilizations are not to be regarded as having intellect, it is obviously too much to expect recognition for the fact that even children in our own culture, not to mention the great majority of the adult population who are remote from academic habits of thought, have minds of their own, which are not necessarily differentiated in the approved manner and yet which are capable of fruitful thought.

Peters seems to regard the particular differentiations which he mentions (but which are not in fact so distinct as he implies, even in their Western academic form) as ends in themselves and not as techniques of abstraction from an essentially integrated world which also lends itself to quite different but equally valid forms of differentiation. He appears to see no difference between the *principle* of differentiation (which we would agree to be essential for thought) and differentiation into the particular categories of a particular segment of a particular culture at a particular historical moment.

The real world is not conveniently divided into history, science, religion, etc., and nor is the mind of a sane, alert person except intermittently and provisionally. History, science and religion are ways of abstracting and examining selected aspects of the world. But the world must nevertheless continue to be *confronted* as an integrated whole. Differentiation and reintegration are continual and continually revised mental activities. That they are not properly recognized as such in formal education accounts for the static and stultifying nature of so much school education. The problems and phenomena that confront us in life are never solely historical or scientific or moral or practical; and neither are our solutions or our ways of experiencing them. The academic traditions do not represent our sole intellectual resources. They are stores or traditions of particular specialized knowledge and criteria (but by no means in themselves unified or consistent) which are justified by the contribution they make to our overall picture of the world. But there is no rational basis for saying that our overall picture is merely the sum of these specializations. The uniting factor, the context of the whole, is ordinary conversation and thought, and since creative, independent activity goes on continually in ordinary conversation and thought without any reference to or necessary derivation from any particular academic discipline, one cannot assume that ordinary thought merely derives from these specializations. On the contrary, the specializations are abstractions from ordinary, common language and thought.

Thus we are not disagreeing with the idea that there is a public language into which the growing member of society is progressively introduced. We are disagreeing with the assumption that, beyond a rudimentary level, this public language is identical with the sum of the academic disciplines. On the basis of such an assumption one would blithely ignore – as formal education frequently and disastrously does – the entire area of intellectual activity that goes on in society at large and which we have mentioned in the previous two chapters.

We have by this time made it clear, we hope, that we are not saying that formal education should merely be a channel for other cultural agencies, formal or informal. We are saying that formal education is a specialized activity which

only has meaning in relation to the public language existing outside itself, and that it must develop its objectives in
this context. The substitution of academic knowledge and
criteria for all knowledge and criteria amounts to a systematic repudiation of the very material – the true common
culture, not 'enshrined' but living and creative – on which,
to be meaningful, the academic component must seek to
operate.

If the common culture of society is not recognized it
will seem only natural to describe children as 'barbarians outside the gates'. Naturally, too, education will be seen as
having no ends beyond itself, for worthwhile existence
hardly appears to go on outside the 'citadel' of education (a
sort of ethereal senior common room) at all.

It is conceded that

> science, mathematics, even history *can* [Peters's italics]
> be viewed in an instrumental way. They contribute to
> hospitals being built and staffed, wars being won, the
> cultivation of the land and to communication across the
> face of the earth. And then what? What are men going
> to do, how are they going to think, what are they going
> to appreciate when their necessary appetites are satis-
> fied? Are these hard men indifferent to all that consti-
> tutes being civilized?

The degree of detachment from the world here claimed
for education is, we must realize, something different from
rational conservatism, which would tend to endorse 'the
cultural canons' as showing the best way to solve the world's
problems, not the best way to ignore them.[5] The material
now 'enshrined' in the academic canons is the result precisely of people attempting to grapple with and solve and
institute their particular solutions to a society's problems
at each stage of its development. This includes 'even' history, religion, literature, for the problems of a society are
not merely cultivation, communication and industry, but
how to conceive of itself, how to agree on policies, what
experiences and environments to value most, and so on.
If the 'canons' are not approached in this spirit but only

as the furnishings of a contemplative citadel, it is no wonder
that vast numbers of students and pupils find them 'irrelevant'. But they are not by any means irrelevant. The understanding of their relevance is merely being prevented by
the false reverence with which their custodians surround
them. To Peters, education appears to be something one
awards oneself *after* one has solved society's problems. If
this point of view were accepted, it might well lead to the
dismantling of the state education system, for why should
society, whose problems, we may take it, are not yet solved,
devote a large proportion of its resources to the maintaining
of a luxury?

Formal education is not initiation. Initiation has already
taken place, through the acquisition of common language,
by the time formal education begins. Formal education,
therefore, is intervention in order to accelerate or widen
processes already begun, and it takes place alongside the
continuing influence of other cultural agencies, to which
it must relate positively, though not uncritically.

In the sciences, education is an attempt to generalize
about the material world; in the arts and social sciences,
about man. Now the subject matter of the arts and social
sciences being man himself, the attempt to generalize is an
attempt to say things which are true about all men, or of
which the truth can be attested by all men. But if it is
something about all men, it is something about which each
man – and child – has unique access to part of the evidence.
Thus no-one's independent testimony can be excluded from
contributing to the sum of knowledge; to which, in any
case, the individual can only gain psychological access
through the paradigm of his own contribution. It is not
good enough to maintain that the canons of worthwhile
knowledge and criteria are 'impersonal'. Taken literally, this
would mean that they are not dependent on people. But
knowledge is intrinsically human – it is created, amassed,
coordinated, criticized, revised and disseminated by people
It is thus not impersonal but multipersonal.

It may be objected that it is absurd to think that in a
classroom discussion an individual pupil who has just read

Hamlet or learnt of the League of Nations for the first time may come up with a new and valid point, or may validly disagree with the accumulated wisdom of hundreds of years' professional literary or historical criticism. The answer is threefold : firstly, there is no logical reason why this should not be the case, since criticism is not a finite exposition of the isolated object or event, but is an interplay of perceptions about the object or event and about contemporary experience; secondly the accumulated wisdom of centuries is an accumulation of disagreements and divergencies, not a systematic whole; thirdly, the pupil is not being confronted with the accumulated wisdom of centuries but by an individual teacher, whose selection from and digestion of the academic sources is very far from being comprehensive or indisputable – as every good teacher will readily acknowledge (and as we describe more fully in chapter 6).

Peters's repeated references to the 'established content' and the 'enshrined canons' of academic disciplines blur the real nature of this content, which embodies all sorts of contending and conflicting concepts. One could maintain that what is 'established' is then not so much particular concepts or views but overall 'rules of debate' between different views and concepts. This makes sense, but only if the rules of debate ultimately lie outside the academic disciplines, since the rules observable within the discipline at any one time are altered by each genuinely new idea adopted into the canon. And of course many of the best ideas, which later become mainstays of the academic discipline, are originally forged outside it, in the course of grappling with a particular problem of the time, and are frequently resisted by Academe until they have lost their controversial currency – that is, their primary impact. The 'rules of debate' are inexplicit and always open to further development; if they are embodied anywhere, it is in common conversation and the entire social situation.

It is possible to argue that the academic disciplines have specialized languages of their own, and that it is this which distinguishes them from ordinary experience and intellect. Certainly the kinds of intensive meaning which they cultivate are a unique contribution to the common culture. But to speak of special languages is to use a metaphor which must not be allowed to run away with us. The 'language' of a discipline is not so much a language as a sub-dialect, dependent on and surrounded by the common language. Even the least obviously dependent dialects such as those of the pure sciences or music are not ways of understanding the world which could conceivably be *alternative* to verbal language – only additional to it. The encompassing language of human wishes and experience is no less than common discourse (sharpened to whatever extent it is by the re-absorption of the special dialects), since no human being who can talk can be excluded from the possibility of having original ideas.

Exaggerated respect for the specialized dialects of the disciplines (as opposed to respect for what has been contributed to the common culture by the use of these dialects) gives rise to the tacit assumption that original thought cannot take place outside them, and a pedantic attribution of every slightly unusual phrase to some authority or other. Original thought may occur in anyone capable of thinking, and becomes current through ordinary discourse. It is only when it reaches academic circles that it gets written down and labelled as someone's property. But it is impossible for anyone to know exactly to what extent his own thoughts are original, since we continually absorb ideas in casual conversation and subconsciously. The world of ideas is by nature a democratic world, and only mystification obscures this.

NOTES

[1] This point was raised by Arnold Downes, 'Values in education', *Rank and File*, 25 (summer 1973).

[2] It is especially on cultural questions that classic Marxists are frequently regarded by libertarians as incorrigible conservatives. Thus while Trotsky maintains that 'mastery

of the art of the past is ... a necessary precondition ... for the building of the new society' ('Culture and socialism', *The Age of Permanent Revolution*, ed. Isaac Deutscher, New York, Dell, 1964) and similar statements were made by Lenin, committed anarchists regard this merely as evidence of subconscious attachment to reactionary values. See for example Anonymous, 'Listen Marxist!', *Anarchos* (USA) (May 1969), reprinted as a pamphlet by Leeds Anarchist Group. The present-day new left often appears to be closer to the anarchists on this question without being aware of it.

[3] See Douglas Holly, 'Crypto-elitists and pseudo-radicals', *The Times Educational Supplement* (26 January 1973), and correspondence in succeeding issues of that journal.

[4] R. S. Peters, 'Education as initiation' in R. D. Archambault (ed.) *Philosophical Analysis and Education* (London, Routledge and Kegan Paul, 1965).

[5] A critique of the work of R. S. Peters as largely an exercise in mystification will be found in D. L. Adelstein, *The Wisdom and Wit of R. S. Peters* (London University Institute of Education Students' Union, 1971).

Chapter 5
Aims

We have concentrated thus far on relations between school and the surrounding culture. We will now, and for the rest of the book, concentrate on the crucial question of the aims of the school. Since the school is a focal point for demands and aspirations from a great variety of lobbies there is no clear agreement on what its priority aims should be, or on whether it can serve an unlimited multiplicity of aims within one institution. In day-to-day practice there is always a degree of pluralism as between subjects, teaching methods and authority styles, but the different practices jostle uneasily together, more or less aware of underlying incompatibilities. At the more generalized level of administrative control and public debate, different rationales contend for the initiative and for the ultimate shaping influence over the school. Mostly without being fully explicit, these rationales, deriving from the perceived interests of different lobbies, weave their way through the debate; and though there is a danger of caricature in trying to distinguish them plainly, it is a danger worth braving if it reveals some of the major chains of reasoning within a ceaseless and often perplexing polemic.

We therefore choose to focus on three such rationales:

education seen as a service to *manpower*, education seen as *the mastery of knowledge* and education seen as a *social service*. These three are selected because they respectively correspond to the perceived interests of three of the most instrumental lobbies which can be distinguished in the arena : industry, the academic establishment and the 'consumers' themselves – the pupils. That these tendencies partially overlap and accommodate each other is plain. But it is equally plain, from the strain between them, that they are by no means happily complementary.

MANPOWER AND KNOWLEDGE

Proponents of the manpower model see the function of education primarily as equipping people to do jobs. It is with this notion foremost in mind that industry and government make their primary assessments of the education system, even though they leave it to the professionals – the academics and administrators – to work out the system in detail, using whatever form of reasoning they feel happiest with. The mastery-of-knowledge model is the one cultivated by academics, and in its purer forms regards education as 'an end in itself' or 'the true reality' or 'the criterion by which all else is judged'. That is to say it regards knowledge as something which is of intrinsic value, of higher value than mere employable skills, which are its by-product, and consequently not in need of justification by its benefits for ordinary economic and social life.

Academics, nevertheless, administer an examination system which has the effect of stratifying the population in a way that employers can make use of. But this effect appears at times to be almost incidental to the academics' point of view. Regarding the pursuit of knowledge as the ultimate reality, many academics tend to look upon the entire examination system as a means of discriminating, through a succession of hurdles, the small minority who are fitted to be of their fraternity. Those who do not get this far are assumed to achieve an element of the good life corresponding to how far along the course they do get. Criticizing the crude utilitarianism of manpower, adherents of knowledge mastery see themselves as defending the intrinsic value of knowledge and the permanent achievements of mankind as against the economic and ideological demands of the age. (R. S. Peters, one of whose essays we considered in the last chapter, would be a representative figure here.)

Critics of this position from the social service angle point out its failure to recognize that the value of given bodies of knowledge changes with changing historical and economic conditions. But this does not mean that the aims of manpower must be paramount. One may hold that knowledge is most meaningful when it can be seen to be useful but that the service of manpower is only one of its uses. Knowledge is useful to people as a resource in every aspect of their predicament.

The boundaries of the disciplines, like those of any individual work of art or science, are essentially provisional when looked at from the point of view of the living person who encounters them, drops them, encounters them again. They define areas which we mentally step into and out of for particular, temporary but recurring, purposes, just as we step into and out of certain clothes or buildings for different purposes. The upholders of knowledge (or education, or art) for 'its own sake', on the other hand, regard the boundaries as permanent and unmodifiable except by the 'professionals' – research workers in universities or elsewhere; and as actually defining reality instead of being created structures for *engaging with* reality, which itself surrounds them and is also perceptible by other means, such as ordinary conversation, popular art or, for that matter, Buddhist contemplation.[1] The true effect of upholding knowledge for its own sake, rather than for people's sake, is to lend a somewhat mystical credence to the *institutions* of education, not to the real content of the subjects, which is in fact malleable and open-ended. Naturally this school of thought is most tempting to some of those whose lives are spent within a specialism in an academic institution.

The content of a discipline is always susceptible to the modifications of scholarship; and the modifications of scholarship are influenced by the entire climate of their times – a climate which is shared by everyone, at whatever depth. There is therefore a relationship, however obscure, between the credibility of a given subject matter with ordinary pupils and the modifications to which that subject matter is liable at the hands of contemporary scholarship. The most audacious and ill-informed judgement made by a pupil on a piece of subject matter with which he is confronted may spring from a similar reaction to that which, at PhD level, is accepted as legitimate new knowledge.

Irrational though it is, the image of knowledge as a commodity is very deeply entrenched in our culture. People appear genuinely to believe that knowledge has an existence apart from human beings. A book is an abstract pattern of marks on the pages until and unless you add the magic catalyst 'concentrating human being'. Of course, we feel as if the knowledge is actually there on the page because the stimulus when we read it is undeniably coming to us from outside ourselves. But in fact the 'out there'-ness of the stimulus is our sense of the presence of the other concentrating human beings who set down the pattern, and also of the other human beings who have concentrated on the same pattern at other times or in other places. There is nothing that adds a sense of vividness to a book so much as coming across someone else's notes in the margin – for a moment there are three of you there concentrating together.

Recorded knowledge is no more than suspended conversation of a highly organized kind. Recorded art is suspended performance. The exceptional intensity of the best of these suspended conversations and performances is attained by the fact that the conditions of the 'conversation' are optimized in certain quite observable and unmysterious ways; we let the other person speak his fill, while we listen hard; he speaks very carefully, thinking out his words for a long time before he says them; there is a temporary boundary of subject matter, allowing intense internal cross-referencing; the conversation is arranged in such a way that we can adjust it exactly to the pace we require, in a way that makes teaching machines look ridiculously crude; finally our awareness of the accessibility of this same suspended conversation to thousands of other people imposes on us an unusual degree of receptive humility, as if we were at a large and very well-ordered public meeting, and this helps us open our minds to new thought. This leaves us still reading the books in a personal way, hearing different emphases from those which others hear (as we realize when we discuss the book with them), but the mental expectancy is radically different from that when, say, we read a personal letter. Additionally, the fact that we have not met the person to whom we are listening means that he must explain himself as fully as possible, taking nothing for granted.

EDUCATION FOR PEOPLE'S SAKE

We have seen, then, that the education system is structured and administered on principles deriving from the view of knowledge as an independent, 'self-governing' pursuit. Timetable, exams, rules, careers are shaped according to academic, not industrial, categories; but the granting and withholding of certificates at various levels stratifies the school population in a way that appears equally to satisfy the perceived needs of employers. The tendency for industrial and professional recruiting to specify entrance requirements in terms of O levels, A levels, ONCs, HNCs, degrees and so forth is, if anything, on the increase.[2]

Turning now to the aims and claims of the third sector, the pupils themselves and the 'social-progressive' teachers and theorists who claim to represent the fuller interests of the pupils, let us see how the administration and ethos of schools is further modified by influence from this quarter. While both 'manpower' and 'knowledge' regard the child instrumentally, the one to serve a pre-defined social need, the other to fulfil a pre-defined intellectual ideal, social progressivism sees the pupils' sense of their own development as the central issue.

A variety of different approaches clusters under this head-

ing. All have some form of child-centredness in common
and are thereby distinguishable from both 'manpower' and
'knowledge'. But not all are equally valid or viable. They
range from the belief that academic authority is no more
than an ideological device for preventing working class
pupils from gaining access to middle class jobs, to the belief
that most working class pupils are intrinsically and irre-
deemably 'non-academic' and therefore should not be
stretched intellectually, merely helped to adjust socially.

It is only the shallower forms of pupil-centred ideology
that regard themselves as self-sufficient alternatives to the
claims of industry and the academic establishment. To
espouse the goal of education for people's sake is in fact
only to raise the question of just how the academic and
industrial influences should be accommodated all the more
acutely. For if we are really interested in 'people's sakes',
we are concerned with everything that we have to face in
life and with every device that may help us face it. The
work situation is the largest and most universal problem,
or complex of problems, faced by us; and the academic
disciplines and their resources are among the most complex
and precise devices for helping us structure what we perceive. Rather than merely jettisoning the existing resources,
we must seek the best way to put the pieces together again
so as to serve a radically different rationale. We must therefore re-examine traditional subjects and their conventional
school presentation to discover their genuine uses from the
pupils' point of view.

GOALS FOR WORKING CLASS PUPILS

There is a good deal of confusion in educational debate between the desire for well-oiled channels to maintain a
'deserving' hierarchy – i.e. to recruit the 'brightest' working
class pupils into the managerial class – and on the other
hand the desire to dissolve the hierarchy itself. To dissolve
the hierarchy means, in the first instance, material equality
in society. Thus Halsey[3] anticipates a situation in which
schools still channel people to different jobs according to

their particular talents but all jobs are equally rewarded. This implies a different rationale for education – in some respects even an opposed one – from that which seeks to give equal opportunity to everyone to get to the top of what is still a pyramid.

The possible attitudes towards the education of the working class could be divided into five:

1 Teach the working class to be working class as the ruling class might be thought to want them to be – 'docile workers', 'subservient', etc.

2 Teach the middle class and neglect the education of the working class.

3 Teach the working class to be as much like the middle class as possible, thereby recruiting into the middle class the few who succeed in crossing the barrier. (Education for individual mobility.)

4 Teach the working class on the assumption that they will stay working class and that therefore different – 'soft' – educational criteria apply to them – i.e. technical competence, leisure interests, social adjustment.

5 Teach the working class assuming that they will stay working class but that they will nevertheless be struggling for equality and for greater fulfilment – as a class.

The prevailing attitude in most secondary schools is some mixture of the first four points. The first point, however, has lost too much credibility to be made explicit often, and the vast bulk of public debate about education takes place on the incomplete spectrum formed by the middle three attitudes. Thus progress would usually be seen as a situation in which working class pupils enjoy school and get something out of it relevant to their realistic job prospects (fourth point); and in which a greater number of the 'brightest' working class pupils go on to higher education while the total higher education population itself nevertheless remains a privileged élite of, say, 10 per cent of the age group (third point); yet in which high resources are still devoted to the education of this élite, and the education of the bulk of working class pupils is therefore still, in practice, rather neglected (second point).

A great weakness of progressive education is that it does not examine the difference between the fourth and fifth propositions. The fourth proposition brings a measure of realism and vigour into secondary education, but on its own may deprive working class pupils of the most valuable educational tools. To adopt the fifth perspective is to appear, in some respects, to come full circle : to believe in giving working class pupils 'hard' educational benefits as well as interest and relevance – not by imposing 'middle class values' on them, nor in the hope that a few of them will become upwardly mobile, but as tools for achieving their own greatest possible fulfilment. The notion of what this fulfilment would extend to is not, then, to be limited, as it tacitly is in many superficially progressive educational concepts, by the assumption that the working class – that is, most people – is, by intellect and temperament, limited to cultural, social and political passivity.

In this (fifth) perspective some of the features of the fourth would also be endorsed. It is necessary to distinguish what might be called the class-transferable elements of 'hard' (traditional, élite) education, such as scientific and philosophical skills, from the class-dependent elements (such as socially exclusive attitudes or historical bias); and to consider the class-transferable elements as part of the resources useful for all pupils. There is every good reason for teaching pupils things which will help them to get and do working class jobs, negotiate bureaucratic channels and the urban environment and so on *and* for teaching them beyond these mere survival skills towards greater self-determination and fulfilment.

When an education derived (in part) from an older ruling class culture is confronted with the objection of irrelevance there are several quite different things that may be intended. A ruling class culture may be irrelevant to a class that is *ruled* – yet not to a class that aspires to *self-rule*. The perceived irrelevance may be a result of the fact that education for working class pupils is so often a feeble *dilution*

and pale *imitation* of a middle class culture of which the
original vigour and critical force has been lost. In this case
the solution is not simply an abandonment of ossified
material in favour of material which reflects immediate circumstances and preoccupations – an ultimately claustrophobic solution to which deschoolers are prone – but a critical
revaluation and recreation of the accumulated as well as
contemporary material *in the light of* present circumstances
and aspirations. It is only the ossified travesty of Shakespeare which is irrelevant to the education of the working
class. The rediscovered, revalued Shakespeare would have a
great deal to say to them.

EQUALITY

The equalization of material benefit in society is outside
the scope of education. It can only be achieved by the
people affected and in the places where they are affected.
Educationists sometimes glibly talk about a rising standard
of living as if this was now automatic; as if the working
class struggles of the past 100 years or more were mere
conformities to some abstract social law, not the conscious
and strenuous struggle of choosing human beings. Formal
education cannot directly participate in this struggle and
cannot decide its progress. But it does inevitably relate to
it, mainly in the degree to which it furnishes all rather
than some people with the tools it has to offer.

It seems unlikely, as we explained in the last chapter, that
schools successfully inculcate attitudes favourable to the
status quo to any depth in working class pupils. There is
to some extent a built-in self-defeating effect in reactionary
education which makes it less likely to 'take'. The educator
who tries to implant support for hierarchy and uncritical
conformity is unlikely to get his ideas across effectively because, by the same token, he has little interest in or respect
for the pupils' own experiences and thoughts. The result for
the pupil is more often frustration and bewilderment than
conviction. The education system does not produce 'docile
workers' as fodder for the entrepreneurs. The whole enter-

prise of schooling is far more confused than that, and in any case frequently fails, whether by reactionary or progressive standards. Its major failing is not that it successfully gives a reactionary education but that it is unsuccessful in educating most pupils at all. The effect of this is by no means progressive, but it hardly makes sense to describe it as positively reactionary either. It is largely a negative effect, which allows other agencies in society to fill the vacuum; and it has this effect, paradoxically, by standing aloof from the other agencies in society and not engaging critically with them.

It is an illusion, of course, to think of the status quo as static, remaining the same so long as it is not positively changed. On the one hand, technological, environmental and commercial change is feverishly pursued by those who are committed to *social* stasis; on the other hand, to repeat old customs, attitudes and educational material without reinvigorating them is also to create something new – a form much more rigid than the original model. The 'culture' purveyed by the schools does not have the virtues which it claims to revere, precisely because those virtues were the virtues of critical vigour when the culture was in the process of formation, and cannot be recovered unless they are recreated from a new standpoint.

The education directly relevant to struggle for higher standards of living is no doubt obtained in the course of struggling, and the relevant skills are probably acquired more in the workplace than anywhere else. This does not mean that formal education is irrelevant to such struggles but that its relevance is indirect. Education influences the person, and the person faces the problems of life, which themselves also educate him. If the lessons of life and work run counter to what is formally taught, they will probably supersede it. What is formally taught must be designed so as to mesh with what is being informally learned outside the school and extend, amplify and constructively criticize it, not to ignore nor suppress, nor yet merely to echo it.

THE HIDDEN POTENTIAL OF SCHOOLS

It would nevertheless be wrong to assume, as some educationists do, that school influence on intellectual attainment is always bound to be fairly marginal. This conclusion reflects the fragmentariness of educational research, which shows that working class pupils on average do not do well in school, no matter what the kind of school. What schools recognize as attainment is only a part of the range of human talents; what researchers recognize as attainment is often even narrower. We know also that schools tend to discriminate (through negative expectations, which act as discouragement) against working class pupils. These three perceptions are rarely put together. Clearly, working class pupils do worse in schools *partly* because the school does not recognize the full range of talents, *partly* because schools themselves discriminate against them and *partly* because material home disadvantages such as low nourishment, crowded space, harassed parents and so on are impediments to ordinary well-being and peace of mind and hence to any autonomous activity including learning. (But these impediments, we should add, do not include 'cultural deprivation' – a very dubious concept, implying that culture is a commodity like bricks and mortar, not the way in which a community interprets and values its experiences.) To resolve these various parts into percentages, as some researchers have done, is somewhat absurd, since the various disadvantages do not add up but *interact*. While a hundred and one independent experiments will show that this, that and the other individual reform does not essentially alter working class disadvantage in schools, this still tells us nothing about what *combination* of reforms *would* alter it, nor does it tell us that such a successful combination is impossible. It may well be that there is a 'take-off' point at which significant and dramatic changes in achievement become possible by means of a thoroughly orchestrated combination of twenty specific reforms none of which on its own, nor any nineteen of which together, make a difference.

The unlikelihood that research will reveal such possibili-

ties is due to its fragmented state, which echoes too easily
the arbitrary categories by which the education system itself is structured: by using divisions of classroom from
classroom, subject from subject, 'method' from 'method' and
so on as definitions of the contours of researchable problems, research fails to reveal the deeper patterns of influence
which would inform a rethinking of the whole educational
experience. The researcher who hopes to identify valuable
reforms by isolating half a dozen classroom variables is like
the individual teacher in his classroom wondering why, having followed all the best advice, he can't get his message
across, when what is actually confounding him is that this
class of pupils has just come out of a negative lesson with
another teacher, is due to go on to yet another teacher in
half an hour, was insulted by the headmaster at the morning assembly, did not get a good breakfast before they
came to school, have been demoralized by failing the eleven
plus, and lost interest in this particular subject over the
course of a year's rapid succession of supply teachers.

To say that no reform can be effective without the positive participation of the class teacher is not to say that the
class teacher really has individual control of the learning
environment. What autonomy he has needs to be defended
to the last ditch, but to fall for the illusion that he can
have genuine control in his own classroom for periods
of three-quarters of an hour at a time arbitrarily sliced out
of a complex and ever-shifting social situation is to lay up
for himself endless frustration. Between individual autonomy and centralized, impersonal direction lies the under-
developed territory of collective teacher responsibility. This
is not a thing which can be achieved by formal statutes,
though it will later be recognized by them, but it is a thing
to which the logic of almost every positive educational reform points, and for which any whole programme of reform cries out.

A major difficulty in implementing education for
people's sake will be to distinguish true changes from
mere changes in rhetoric or packaging. You can call a
school 'comprehensive' by putting it in a single building

which in effect maintains a grammar section and a secondary modern section side by side; you can adopt a different speechday jargon, emphasizing 'creativity' and 'socialization' yet remain repressive in blow-by-blow classroom relationships; you can pass staffroom resolutions, or fill researchers' questionnaires, supporting positive discrimination for the disadvantaged, yet still devote disproportionate resources to the A level candidates at the expense of the others.

We must beware, therefore, of overestimating the extent and depth of changes in educational practice. Nevertheless, schools are undoubtedly different places now from what they were as little as fifteen years ago. And as it becomes clear that an education system cannot, on its own, satisfy the desires of a community for redistribution of earning power, let alone of wealth in general, the school is increasingly focused on as a destination in itself, a place where we may spend as much as a sixth of our lives; a place therefore where criteria of direct satisfaction should be applied, rather than a place which must justify itself entirely by its effectiveness as a preparing ground for other areas of life.[4]

Superimposing on this the idea of permanent education – the idea that one's entitlement to education may be spread out intermittently throughout one's adult life; adding also a gradually widening view of the range of alternative human talents; and also the notion of the school as a resource centre for the local community – putting all these things together, the picture emerges of a future school which would be the focal point of local cultural and social life in a way that churches once were in village communities, only reflecting more varied inspirations and a more self-conscious collective autonomy.

The value of such a role for the school would be all the greater for the realization that it would to some extent alleviate the impact of the more stressful and dehumanizing features of contemporary life. Impersonality, lack of community, is a hallmark of so many of our workplaces, leisure places and shopping places. Our architecture, both commercial and residential, expresses *ad nauseam* the principle of identical repeated units. Our factories, our offices, our supermarkets and our cinemas are places where we are processed in hordes without really meeting. Only some of our newer theatres and community centres show the way towards what our schools could be if the culture of which they are custodians were restored to living currency.

Once again, however, acceptance of this community-centred prospect for schools does not automatically dispose of the question of what value to attach to, and what use to make of, their traditional resources. Rather it raises this question in an even more pressing form. To emphasize the measure of client satisfaction is not to abandon aims of intellectual mastery or cultural growth, for the clients themselves will aspire to such achievements more, not less keenly, as barriers of mystique and disqualification are removed.

We must therefore look very closely at the structure of the traditional curriculum to see which of its features are virtues that would need to be retained and developed in a fully progressive school system, and which would be impediments to the creation of such a system. The next chapter is devoted to this question.

At the same time we need to look equally closely at current attempts to rationalize the aim of knowledge mastery by the use of curriculum evaluation methods, and again ask in what respects these methods are a help or a hindrance to the realization of progressive aims. That is the subject of chapter seven.

NOTES

[1] Alan Watts, *Nature, Man and Woman* (London, Thames and Hudson, 1958), explores the case for the non-conceptual nature of our primary awareness of reality.

[2] See Asa Briggs and A. G. Watts, 'Are your A-levels really necessary?', *The Sunday Times Magazine* (7 October 1973).

[3] 'The selective function of education for a hierarchy of

occupational positions would be transformed into one of differentiation for a complex and fluid array of jobs having roughly equal material rewards', A. H. Halsey, 'Socialism and educational opportunities', *The Times Higher Educational Supplement* (8 June 1973).

⁴ See Christopher Jencks *et al.*, *Inequality : a reassessment of the effect of family and schooling in America* (London, Allen Lane, 1973); and see more particularly the discussion of the book by Phillip W. Jackson *et al.* and the reply by Christopher Jencks in 'Perspectives on *Inequality*', *Harvard Educational Review*, 43 (1) (February 1973) (Cambridge, Mass., USA).

Chapter 6
Curriculum structure

LESSONS AND SUBJECTS

The basic unit around which secondary schools are structured is the lesson – one lesson in one subject with one class. It is easy to see that the lesson unit is in many ways artificial. But then, so is any form of focusing on some aspects of knowledge to the exclusion of others. And any sustained thinking whatever involves just such a focusing. It does not, therefore, get us very far to say that boundaries such as subjects and lessons should simply be swept away. For every time we decide to concentrate for some length of time on a topic that interests or has relevance for us we are establishing a boundary of some kind between that topic and all the other aspects of the world which are equally liable to impinge on us and claim our attention.

School subjects derive their names and are supposed to derive their value from academic disciplines – subjects cultivated in universities. The traditional school timetable is often defended in terms of the value of the academic disciplines as authoritative bodies of knowledge in which teachers are experts. But there is a great distance between lessons – that is, school subjects as actually presented – and the academic disciplines. You cannot argue from the value of the disciplines to the value of the traditional timetable, because so many other things come into account in the timetable, and the success or failure of lessons depends to a large extent on these other things.

The supposed boundary of the discipline is only one boundary used in the organization of learning in the school. Others are the school itself, the class, the classroom, the lesson, the individual teacher, the limits of the teacher's knowledge, and the particular objectives adopted by this teacher for this lesson with this class. The most important thing is the cogency of the lesson itself, and of the sequence of lessons (both the sequence in the course of a day and the sequence of lessons in a particular subject).

The claims made for the disciplines are frequently contrasted with the activities of other agencies, often viewed with hostility, such as 'peer group subcultures', 'influence of the mass media' and 'home background'. The implication is that if the claims of the discipline to be conceptually superior to other influences on children are upheld, the school is justified in requiring pupils to suspend their other preoccupations and absorb the offered subject matter.

We have pointed out in earlier chapters that this represents firstly a gross undervaluation of the conceptual content of the informal educational influences (home, mass media, colloquial talk and so on); and secondly a failure to see that the academic disciplines meet the informal influences in a continuum, influence and are influenced by them, and form a single culture with them. What we want to concentrate on in this chapter is the imprecision in the assumption that school subjects reproduce the virtues of the academic disciplines. The implication is not that school subjects and lessons are superfluous but that, to be of value, they must be intellectually cogent in themselves, not by reference to some 'higher' stage of learning which, for most pupils, is never reached.

The thing that formal education has to offer that the pupil is least likely to get adequately from the informal circulation of knowledge in society is practice in *coordinating* forms of thought and lines of inquiry. This reflects the academic disciplines at a much deeper level than that which sees them simply as sources of authoritative knowledge. Knowledge, interpretation and evaluation are all susceptible to change; if the disciplines are valuable *across* changes of this kind, if they are valuable despite the fact that there are many disagreements within them and that one generation of scholars often turns the work of its predecessors upside down, their value is surely not so much in particular facts and concepts as in the skills of coordinating facts and concepts which they practise.

Enlightened educators have often pointed out that the most lasting thing a pupil can learn is how to learn. In fact, the continuing encounter with informal education, the general circulation of ideas in the common culture, and changes in environment and circumstances ensure that, with a merely natural wakefulness, we continue to learn. But what may more easily be lost is the faculty of coordinating what we learn; of sustaining a network of concepts which permit extensive comparison and evaluation of the many things we have known. This requires sustained focus on particular subject matter.

Traditional education tends to regard lessons in academic subjects as fragments of a grand design to initiate pupils, step by step, into the edifice of the disciplines. The majority of pupils, of course, drop out, or are dropped out, somewhere along the line. The conventional view is that this is because the concepts get too difficult for them. Ignoring the fact that the cut-off points in schooling (eleven plus, CSE, O level, A level) are determined by social and economic rather than educational reasoning, the traditional educationist regards the progressive elimination of four-fifths of the population from formal education as simply so much natural and necessary wastage.

The major wastage, however, has not been that these pupils did not stay on at school but that the courses which they took were not designed to make sense and be satisfying in themselves. If they had been, it would have been seen that far more pupils were interested in and capable of 'intellectual' attainment.

The assumption that, in 'academic' subjects, lessons and courses at earlier stages of learning are essentially preparations for the later stages prevents the educator from focusing clearly on the need to ensure that the earlier courses make sense in themselves. 'In themselves' does not of course mean in isolation but in relation to the informal educational context of society at large – the common culture. One might propose that there should be internal evidence of the value of what is learnt at least within periods of, say, a term at a time. By internal evidence is meant the pupil's corroboration that what he has learnt has made reality more visible, more manageable to him in some way.

There are already, of course, 'terminal' courses of various kinds designed for school leavers. But the assumption in the design of these courses is usually that they cannot have more than a rudimentary intellectual content. They are courses 'for the non-academic pupil'.[1] We are talking of something altogether more ambitious: courses with intensive and satisfying intellectual content but designed as relatively self-contained units.

But if such courses are viable, they would also be an immense improvement for the 'academic' pupil, whose greater conventional success at school does not necessarily indicate that the courses he takes make any more immediate sense to him. Part of his 'academic' aptitude is the aptitude to persist with intellectual puzzles which he still has not internalized. The difference in his motivation from that of the school leaver may be in his greater avidity for qualifications, his greater willingness to defer intellectual judgement or his greater wish for the approval of teachers. But he is not necessarily more independent-minded nor more able to relate what knowledge he has to the world of his experience. It is a problem for teachers in higher education that many of their students are intellectually timid, unwilling to use their own judgement, unwilling to question the authority of a book, unable, therefore, to transform their supposed intellectual advantage into real mental currency. Of course, the same characteristics may be found in many lecturers themselves. Higher education presents, in fact, the

two opposite problems in counterpoint – students whose
independent-mindedness is felt as a threat by lecturers who
fear having their own confusion exposed; and independent-
minded lecturers whose students cannot, after thirteen years
of success through intellectual conformity, grasp that they
are being asked to think for themselves.

THE GAP BETWEEN DISCIPLINES AND LESSONS

The following points need to be kept in mind when there
is any question of justifying a lesson or course of lessons
by reference to an academic discipline:

A discipline is not an entity with visible boundaries. It
may contain many contradictory points of view. It is not a
steady accumulation of authentic material; whatever it has
accumulated in the way of literature, criticism, documents,
evidence, theories and so on is always open to revaluation
and reinterpretation. In fact revaluation and reinterpretation
are going on the whole time, and they are influenced by
the whole of contemporary culture and society, not just by
developments within the discipline itself.

Even if we still retain the idea of a discipline as an area
of knowledge with approximate borders, no individual has
digested the whole of it. The teacher has made a personal
synthesis of selected elements of a discipline. But a teacher
is sometimes himself alienated from his own discipline. He
may find himself teaching things which he himself doesn't
understand but has taken on trust in his own education. He
may mistakenly think of the discipline as a body of un-
changing knowledge, and may be unable to cope with new
ideas in the subject arising from pupils' reactions, even
though the discipline 'itself' is susceptible to new ideas at
the level of, say, university research – or anywhere within
it where original thought is welcomed. And of course with
a given class at a given time, a teacher does not present even
his own synthesis and selection from the discipline but only
a small selection from that selection.

Neighbouring disciplines which constantly refer to each
other (such as literature and history) will be represented to

pupils by different teachers who may not have coordinated their work in any way; and even the same discipline may be represented to pupils by different teachers, with different syntheses from it, who may or may not have coordinated their ideas on the subject. Finally, over the length of a secondary school pupil's career, the teachers representing each discipline are likely to change a number of times. In a bad situation they may change frequently, even several times a year (where the position is filled by supply teachers).

The high incidence of teacher turnover that is now common argues perhaps for the establishment, where at all possible, of universally applicable stages in the learning of a discipline, so that a minimal continuity of subject matter can be secured across a scene of changing teacher populations. It also argues for within-school and regional coordination of teaching objectives in each subject to be a regular part of the work of schools, with timetabled planning time. Techniques of coordinating teacher approach and subject matter with other teachers should be devised and built into teacher training programmes. They would need to be on a democratic model, responsive to the influence of all participating teachers, to prevent the arbitrary imposition of overall plans which may be unrealistic for particular classes or teachers.

Nevertheless, the number of variables which would need to be coordinated to establish definite stages of learning over a five- or seven-year period in any given discipline would be so great that it would be futile to think that such measures could be firmly established. It is also by no means certain that there are definite sequences of learning stages which all pupils must pass through, rather than a vast variety of alternative routes from some simple concepts to other complex ones. The curriculum evaluation approach (the conceptual analysis that would be necessary to find the 'stages') must be complemented by recognizing the importance of ensuring that relatively small course units – units of a year, a term or less – make sense to pupils in themselves. Rather than stressing the attempt to 'initiate'

pupils into bodies of knowledge which are mistakenly con-
ceived of as static edifices, the primary objective of teaching
should be to re-create the *primary* virtues of 'disciplined'
thinking, namely ability to structure complex subject matter and to sustain extensive networks of reference points
and concepts.

The difference may appear at first sight abstract and unimportant, but in practice it is significant. The assumption
that disciplines are authoritative bodies of knowledge and
that lessons are bits of disciplines is the myth sustaining a
marvellously fragmented and aimless timetable. Continuity
of content and focus is vested in the *teacher*, identified with
the subject that he teaches all day, all year. Pupils, on the
other hand, are given a ceaseless succession of piecemeal
tasks of totally different kinds. Everything works against
their being able to make extended connections between what
they have learned in the strung-out sequence of lessons allocated to a subject. At best the teacher has a year-long or
term-long plan; at worst he too is living from lesson to
lesson. To pupils, the units which make up the year's or
term's plan are separated by long periods filled with equally
fragmentary pieces of other subjects. The school's lack of
interest in shaping meaningful learning situations is ab-
sent-mindedly justified by the assumption that the content
of each lesson is an authentic excerpt from a worthwhile
body of knowledge. Little attention is paid to the effect of
adjacent lessons on each other or of the rapidity with which
authority figures, authority styles, subject terminology and
classroom environments change. In short, everything con-
spires against the element of sustained focus passing over
from teachers to pupils. The whole merry-go-round, indeed,
is designed on the assumption of a norm of intellectual passivity and motivational untrustworthiness in the pupils. They
must be supervised and kept occupied at all times. They
must absorb history in the history lesson, English in the
English lesson, maths in the maths lesson and chemistry in
the chemistry lesson; and the moment at which they must
cease to absorb the one and begin to absorb the next is arbitrated for them by a mechanical plan which is totally

divorced from the internal logic of the subject matter or the internal rhythm of their own concentration.

The inflexibility of this system is not insuperable. Some degree of the sensitivity of primary school timetabling, in which a balance of activities is aimed at, should be imported into the secondary school. With the advent of other reforms, especially team teaching, integrated studies and middle schools, the opportunities for better timetabling also improve. For example, where a team of teachers have a year-group divided between them and take different groups within it alternately, it is possible for the times of lessons to be modified from day to day by agreement among the teachers, without the rest of the school being affected.

THE NATURE OF CONCENTRATION

To understand what value the lesson, fixed or flexible, might have for pupils as a basis for sustained focus, we must take carefully into account the nature of that mental coordination which we are trying to encourage. What exactly is going on in a person when he is engaged in work on a scientific theory, a historical study, a play or a novel? What happens to his 'ordinary' self and to the thousand impressions of ordinary life which make up his consciousness? And, apart from the hypothetical boundary drawn around the subject, what is the influence of the secondary boundaries which are established ostensibly to support the primary one in a school or college – boundaries of career, timetable, institution, finance, role and so on?

The everyday world of colloquial speech and ordinary impressions is never, of course, wholly banished when we are reading a book, writing an essay, watching or acting in a play, studying, developing a theory or any other such conspicuously 'educational' activity. The outside world is only suspended and subdued, and that only temporarily. We are aware of it at the back of our minds, and it rises and falls in our consciousness as we are reminded of one thing and another by the material on which we are consciously concentrating. If this were not the case, in fact, it would be impossible for us to make sense of the thing on which we are concentrating, since it is composed of elements many of which are drawn either more or less directly from the everyday world and from other disciplines. There is a two-way system of comparison operating all the time, somewhere at the threshold of consciousness, between the matter on which we are concentrating and the pool of reference points from the world of our experience. On the one hand we 'refer' to the reference points in order to understand the material; on the other, the material reinforces the reference points which it calls into play, adds to them and suggests new patterns of organization for them.

We play a sort of willing trick on ourselves by which we focus on an external set of symbols, seeming thereby to forget ourselves and our previous preoccupations; but we do so in order to bring into play those parts of ourselves and our preoccupations which are generally skated over in the constant shifting-of-focus of hourly activity. By the effort to create or absorb a pattern of symbols 'out there', we improve the organization of symbols 'in here', 'inside' our heads. 'Out there' also means in common with other people, and our confidence that what is 'out there' is also seen or seeable by other people is a vital part of that sense of reality which this activity serves to cultivate.

The store of personal reference points which the concentrating person brings to his scrutiny of the new material is an essential catalyst in making the new material cohere for that individual. But since subjects do not exist independent of human beings, each person's encounter with them alters them in some way at that time (whether or not the alteration is recorded or transmitted and so persists for other people).

The fact that subject matter can be altered by the person who is concentrating on it is admitted at the 'highest' levels.

> ... The ultimate mystery of the subject is revealed very late in the educational life. By the ultimate mystery, I mean its potential for creating new realities ... the ultimate mystery of the subject is not coherence but inco-

herence; not order but disorder; not the known but the unknown.[2]

But while debate between the disciplines and contemporary life is sanctified at academic levels as research, the rest of the education system tends to treat the subjects as closed systems, as 'the real', 'the valuable' and 'the permanent', as if they were *alternative* to the pupils' ordinary perceptions. But the pupils' perceptions reflect, at their own level, those same forces of contemporary experience which are the source of 'legitimate' modifications of knowledge at the research level.

Pupils can never truly put aside all thought of their own lives and preoccupations in order to concentrate on a particular subject. Concentration does not work like that. It is much subtler. There must be an encounter between the new subject matter and the prior content of the pupil's mind. This implies the activation of both. The exclusion of other thoughts from the forefront of the pupil's mind is always a balancing act. And so the common plea for relevance in schoolwork should be understood not necessarily as a wish for topical subject matter but for more of the relevance of received subject matters to be demonstrated or made discoverable. This, of course, makes greater demands on the teacher than merely the abandonment of all established subject matter. It requires the teacher himself to be capable of revaluating, or of guiding a revaluation of, complex subject matter in the light of contemporary life. It requires him to be independent-minded towards his own higher education – not a faculty which teacher education is renowned for developing.

THE VALUE OF STRUCTURE

The structure of subjects is a reflection of the nature of mental concentration, not of the world direct. They are the record of past thinking. Any form of thought is a form of focusing; and any focusing means concentrating on selected features of the total visible or thinkable environment to the exclusion of others. The exclusion (at surface level) is as important as the inclusion. Thus every form of thinking involves a boundary of some kind and some duration. The disciplines from which school subjects derive their names are merely particular traditions of sustained focusing, and therefore of temporarily excluding other forms of thought. The value of such forms of focusing, and of establishing them as permanent conventions which can be stepped into and out of, is that they make possible a more intense internal organization of symbols (facts, ideas, concepts, definitions, images) than can usually be maintained in the flow of ordinary life, with its constantly shifting focus.

The world is not divided into subjects or disciplines. We cannot assume that it is divided at all – except through the operation of our minds. The capacity of the mind to pick out the shape of an event or a fact from the environment, to distinguish figure from ground, is prior to the existence of subjects. Subjects are extensions of this basic faculty. We can see and speak of a car crash or a marriage or an argument, and relate them to other events of the same kind, without placing them in a recognized subject. The disciplines abstract particular aspects of phenomena and build up traditions of thought around them. Thus a car crash, a marriage or an argument has a chemical aspect, a physical aspect, a biological aspect, a historical aspect, a moral aspect, a religious aspect, etc. History is the abstraction of the historical aspect of the car crash and the marriage and the argument, and everything else in the world; biology of the biological aspect, and so on. Thus the value of subjects is in part derived from their withdrawal from the immediate pressures of shifting focus. But this withdrawal is never complete, never a withdrawal of all levels of a person's consciousness. Nor does it last continuously for more than, at most, a few hours at a time.

Works of art and fiction are good examples of networks of symbols around which a boundary has been placed in order to facilitate intense internal cross-referencing. The intense imaginative effect of a film or play, like the concentrated reasoning of a scientific or historical theory, is made possible by deliberate suspension of involvement in the harrying circumstances of ordinary life. We see the rudiments of this clearly in the semi-formal techniques of ordinary conversation – telling jokes for example. If you want to know the point of a joke you have to be quiet and listen for the few moments that it takes to tell it. The symbol system in a joke is of course relatively simple. Often it is the relationship between a norm and an idiosyncratic deviation from the norm – 'An Englishman, an Irishman and a Scotsman ...', 'So he said to the first one, he said to the second one, he said to the third one ...'. In the common three-people or three-incidents pattern, the first two are there to define the significance to be attached to the third. Without the care given to the defining of the context and terms of reference, so to speak, the anecdote would be unintelligible.

Plays, films, stories, poems rest on more elaborate patterns of this kind. What we mean when we say that it takes us the first ten minutes to 'get into' a narrative is that it takes us this amount of time to absorb the primary 'definitions', the mapping out of reference points, which enable us to interpret the later symbols (not so much *what* they symbolize, which can always be argued about, but what relative weights to attach to them).

Subjects are yet more elaborate symbol systems but their boundaries are in many ways less firm than those of works of art. Their appearance of having a permanent and separate life of their own comes from the fact that educational institutions and careers are established in their name. In reality the subjects are still no more than the sum of mental activities of a certain kind practised by people anywhere at any time, plus the record of such activities practised by people in the past. These activities always take place in the context of ordinary life and the common culture. Different subjects are distinguished by having their own special terminology and their favoured subject matter, and by the kinds of questions that they ask. Yet no subject could exist only on concepts or subject matter peculiar to itself.[3] Its favoured material is set in a common language without which it would be inaccessible. And when a subject coins new terminology or concepts, or produces new subject matter, these in turn become (or are liable to become) part of the common culture.

The apparent objective existence of subjects, the way in which they have been made to seem independent of the human mind, is in fact a projection of the human mind – a valuable projection, much as the artist projects the content of his mind onto paper or canvas so that he can operate on it, developing his imagery *by* working on the picture. *Law* makes another good paradigm. It is written down as unambiguously as possible. What is written down is the record of shared understandings and is intended thereafter to govern behaviour. By reference to it we take decisions, imprison each other and so on. Yet it is only at root a function of human relationships. It is made by human beings and does not exist independent of them. It only makes sense in a context which it does not wholly control and which in fact controls it. In reality there are only relationships and decisions, and the record of relationships and decisions; and relationships and decisions continue their own development outside the law as well as through it. Essentially the law can only govern behaviour so long as behaviour finds it useful to govern itself through the law. Similarly, subjects can only discipline intellect so long as intellect finds it beneficial to discipline itself through subjects.

What are the implications of all this for the structuring of lessons and courses? Not, by any means, that structure is superfluous. The apparent drift of progressive education away from structure is a reaction against the arbitrary structure imposed by the teacher who requires pupils to imitate piecemeal fragments of the structure of knowledge in *his* mind, instead of inducing the development of sustained structures in *their* minds. The illusion that traditional education is well organized *educationally* is produced by the fact that the teacher can see the structure of the term's or week's work. What the pupils experience is a series of arbitrary demands. Not only the content but the form of the tasks given, and of the criteria applied to their fulfilment, is commonly that of an arbitrary demand, belonging to the wishes of the teacher rather than the nature of the subject matter: I want you to do such and such; I am not satisfied with this piece of work; I found your essay interesting. Harold Rosen shows that this makes a fundamental difference to the pupil's orientation to the subject matter of his task. Schools should 'produce writers who have developed the capacity to generate their own reasons for writing and to define their own audiences which should include those which are large in number and unknown'; but in fact the teacher 'initiates the writing ... by defining a writing task (and) also nominates himself as audience. He is not, however, simply a one-man audience but also the sole arbitrator, appraiser, grader and judge of the performance.'[4]

FRUITFUL DEVIATIONS

The problem for the teacher is to devise situations in which students are led to create for themselves sustained structures of thinking rather than merely trying to master extracts of prestructured subject matter. In fact, genuinely to digest any kind of subject matter, however prestructured, is always to recreate it for oneself, probably changing it to some extent in the process. Thus perhaps the art of pupil-centred teaching lies more in the encouragement and facilitation of autonomous intellectual activity *around* well-structured (and well-chosen) subject matter than in putting too much emphasis on the ability of pupils to arrive at satisfactory themes, topics and problems through the sheer exercise of curiosity and creativity. It may be that at the core of teaching will remain the encounter with structured selections from disciplines – *more* carefully selected and structured than in traditional education. But there will be less emphasis on the need to master the precise surface form of such selections and far more on the variety of avenues of thought which can be opened up around them, and from which one would periodically return to the given

subject matter or a variation on it with deepened appreciation. The teacher will have thoroughly prepared his subject matter in the light of his previous knowledge of the
pupils, but will also be alert to any deviations from the
prepared ground which might prove fruitful. A fruitful
deviation would be a 'sidetracking' arising when pupils'
reactions to the material with which the teacher confronts
them leads in a different direction from that catered for in
his prepared objectives. The capacity to take unexpected
opportunities and recognize the value of some kinds of
'distraction' is of course something which good teachers
have always had. A great deal of bad teaching consists in
not recognizing and not exploiting fruitful deviations, or
indeed in penalizing them.

Deviations will be of various kinds. Some will fall within
the area of the given discipline (for example, one may as
easily demonstrate the concept of historical causality or
literary influence with one set of events or authors as with
another). Others will fall into the area of another recognizable discipline, and the teacher's capacity to handle them
will be a matter of luck. Clearly, the implications of regarding pupil-initiated deviations as legitimate are that the
teacher's role as expert is publicly diminished. A correspondingly franker relationship with the pupils is essential,
and a more reciprocal, less isolated, relationship with
teachers in other disciplines is indicated.

Further deviations will not fall neatly into a recognizable
discipline area at all. It would be a useful exercise to try
to devise a set of criteria by which fruitful deviations might
be recognized. This would require empirical observation of
a great many lessons, as well as theoretical analysis; here
we can only suggest some types of deviation which might
serve as rudimentary classifications.

Those falling within the same discipline might be divided
into 'short cuts', 'detours' and 'changes of destination',
according to their relationship to the teacher's prearranged
objectives (which themselves would have been influenced
by deviations that had proved fruitful in previous lessons).
Those falling within another discipline would be admissible

or not depending on the particular teacher's talents and confidence.

An example of a non-discipline-bound deviation might be collective discussion 'for its own sake' – that is, for some such objective as the development of articulacy irrespective of subject matter; or for the development of social relationships; or even simply as mental therapy – the relief and social validation of painful preoccupations. All these are valid objectives in themselves; all are aids to other learning as well.

FOCUSING

Given the rigid nature of traditional teaching, it is not surprising that progressive education should have opened its arms enthusiastically to any 'deviation' – to any enthusiasm or interest on the pupils' part at all. But given the endless possibilities of deviation, and deviation from deviation, what sort of principles can a teacher employ to retain some structure and direction in his teaching?

The problem is best understood as one of focusing. Where subject matter is wholly open-ended, focusing becomes extremely difficult. If the principle of fruitful deviations is exercised, there is correspondingly less danger that the teacher's initial selection of material will become too rigid. A bold selection of material is therefore possible. The teacher cannot escape from the fact that the initiative rests with him. This is the nature of the role and the institution, and would still apply even if attendance at school were voluntary. The 'audience' is attracted (or the pupils' attendance compelled) with the promise that something of value will be offered to them. The teacher is aware that what he offers may be inappropriate. Even where this is the case, the appropriate thing may only be able to be discovered by the pupils' reactions to the inappropriate – i.e. by fruitful deviations. To put the *initial* onus for focusing on the pupils themselves may cause bafflement and frustration.

The presentation of structured subject matter accompanied by willingness to deviate from it thus has a psycho-

logical value as well as an intellectual one. Whether because
of the prevalence of traditional teaching or because, insti-
tutionally, initiative rests inescapably with the teacher,
pupils tend to have an expectation that they are going to be
required to do something that the teacher will specify.
Once pupils' interest is fully engaged, their own motivation should prove sufficient to keep a task afloat for a period
of time. But so long as it is seen by teachers as provisional,
as representing the pupils' own motivation which has been
projected onto the teacher, there is no danger to progressive aims in the teacher's being strongly directive for limited
periods. Indeed if he fails to be so he may incur frustration
among pupils who expect it of him. But his directives should
weaken as the pupils' autonomous motivation strengthens
– as would have been his intention from the start.

Another virtue of an alternation of structured material
and unstructured deviations is that it corresponds to the
necessary interdependence, the complementary ebb and
flow, of 'convergent' and 'divergent' thinking.[5] The popu-
larization of these categories has sometimes led to the conclusion, in our view superficial, that individuals may be
better suited to scientific disciplines if they have convergent
tendencies or to the humanities if divergent. Any fruitful
intellectual act requires the use of both convergent and
divergent faculties, though not necessarily simultaneously
or in the form 'What is the correct answer to X?' nor in
the form 'Think of as many answers to X as you possibly
can' (the two forms used in convergent and divergent tests).
The natural form in which problems make themselves felt is:
'Firstly, what is the problem (which is causing the
disjunction I now perceive in reality)?; and secondly, what
is the *optimum feasible* answer to that problem?' The
equipment necessary to identify and solve the problem consists of both the convergent and divergent faculties, used
alternately : the convergent faculty to differentiate the
problem from its context; the divergent to conceive all
the possible solutions; the convergent again to judge which
solutions are feasible; the divergent again to conceive
all the advantages and disadvantages of the various feasible

courses of action; and the convergent again to select the optimum.

To assume that people with a strong tendency in one or other direction ought to pursue an educational course which will lead to an occupation making maximum use of that tendency not only encourages uncritical acceptance of the norm of specialized occupations but underestimates the complexity of intellectual processes in any one discipline or occupation.

The theory of the two faculties arose from the suspicion that schooling favoured convergent thinking and failed to recognize the value of divergent thinking; that is, that there was a tremendous overemphasis on correct answers. This suspicion was abundantly justified. Having recognized the value – more particularly the *interdependent* value – of both, schooling must not only give opportunity to and recognition for the exercise of either, but must attempt to help pupils to develop the complementary faculty to that towards which they lean.

Most people have observed about themselves or others that often they are best able to 'diverge' when they have something concrete to diverge *from*. A person who feels lost if confronted with the task of explaining the First World War may be able to produce a very divergent performance when reacting against the *convergent* task of naming three contributory causes to that war. He may then, and only then, be able to produce *six* 'causes' – or he may only then be able to state clearly, 'It is impossible to distinguish three causes, since all causes were intermingled', and go on to produce a highly integrated (i.e. convergent-cum-divergent) account of the subject.

The mechanism is similar to that whereby, dithering over a decision, we need someone else's definite advice one way or the other, whether we take it or not, in order to discover our own mind. Putting a boundary around something enables one to structure what is outside it as well as what is inside, if only initially by the fact of its exclusion.

What we have been trying to show in this section is that structured subject matter is served just as well, if not better, by progressive teaching; and that the flexibility of approach required by pupil-centred teaching is susceptible of fairly close description and is not (or ought not to be) a mere prescription for vagueness. This flexibility includes recognition of the value of objectives other than the purely intellectual, both in themselves and as prerequisites for fruitful learning – objectives that would loosely be called social : therapeutic self-expression, the mutual socialization of a group, the building up of self-confidence, and so on. But it also includes recognition of the necessity for providing a number of alternative channels even for directly intellectual objectives – alternative routes to the highly articulated thought-constructs which remain the most valuable fruit of intellectual attainment.

NOTES

[1] Michael F. D. Young, 'On the politics of educational knowledge', *Economy and Society*, 1 (2) (1972) (published by Routledge and Kegan Paul), argues that the provision of special courses for the 'non-academic' pupil is part of the schools' negative discrimination against working class pupils.

[2] Basil Bernstein, 'On the classification and framing of educational knowledge' in Earl Hopper (ed.), *Readings in the Theory of Educational Systems* (London, Hutchinson, 1971), pp. 195-6.

[3] See Kathryn P. Morgan, 'Some philosophical difficulties concerning the notion "structure of a discipline"', *Educational Theory*, 23 (1) (1973) (published by the University of Illinois).

[4] Harold Rosen, 'Written language and the sense of audience', *Educational Research*, 15 (3) (1973), p. 181.

[5] See Liam Hudson, *Contrary Imaginations* (London, Methuen, 1966).

Chapter 7
Selection and evaluation

Of the three educational aims distinguished in chapter five
– manpower, mastery of knowledge and social progress –
it is social progress, we have implied, that should form the
cornerstone of a new perspective for education. In this
perspective the other two aims would be reinterpreted, not
rejected. Although progressive aims have been gaining
credibility over the past decade in particular, they have
gained serious ground in those areas of the education system
that are of least direct concern to adherents of the manpower and knowledge aims. The further up the school system you go towards the critical structure points of O and
A level the smaller the effect of the progressive criteria and
the more entrenched the reign of the knowledge/manpower
axis.

Progressive reforms proved viable first in primary schools,
then in dismantling the early structuring point of the know-
ledge/manpower rationale, the eleven plus exam – but not
without intense resistance, which still continues; and now
among some younger age groups and less able pupils in
secondary schools. Meanwhile industry and the professions
have been attaching progressively more importance to paper
qualifications, or the lack of them, and curriculum theorists

have been devoting sophisticated statistical analysis to increasing the efficiency of school examinations in their own terms.[1]

The origins of new educational ideas are too manifold to pin down; but one can distinguish their respective significance to some extent by looking at their patronage. The main 'customers' for progressive education are teachers who feel that traditional educational practice does not get through to their pupils, particularly working class pupils. As they face the pupils every day, direct apprehensions of pupil interest and involvement are foremost in their minds. A more abstract view of knowledge and a greater concern with selection, qualifications and manpower prevail at the administrative levels.

USES OF TESTS

Innovations to do with education have some appeal to both levels, but for different reasons. The term 'evaluation' as used by curriculum theorists usually means measurement by means of some kind of test. Educational testing may have a number of different purposes – diagnosis of particular pupils' weaknesses, assessment of whether particular objectives have been attained, assessment of individual pupil attainment on 'standardized' criteria (comparison with a national norm), and assessment for selection purposes.[2] Testing is also the principal instrument, as well as largely the product, of educational research.

Of these various purposes, selection and standardization of attainment have most appeal to the knowledge/manpower axis, while diagnosis and course evaluation have most practical use for teachers. As a tool for the use of teachers, 'curriculum evaluation' represents an attempt to rationalize the process of teaching itself – its objectives and its ways of judging whether these objectives have been attained.[3] The methods proposed hold a certain degree of promise and also have certain limitations which we will go into in a moment. But it is selection to which most testing is devoted – even when the tests are ostensibly for purposes of diagnosis or checking objectives. Together with public examinations, this emphasis on increasing the efficiency of selection and rejection represents an attempt by the knowledge/manpower axis to rationalize its aims.

Thus the pattern of development over the past decade is not properly appreciated if we notice only the growth of the social-progressive practices, for this growth has not been at the expense of knowledge/manpower aims. Rather, both parties have been developing their techniques, progressives from the bottom of the system upwards (in both age and 'ability' terms), knowledge/manpower from the top downwards. At the present time they have virtually met in the middle, the demarcation line being in effect the Certificate of Secondary Education exam. For the CSE is the first public educational examination which has been designed to be passed by a *majority* of the age group, and which has been seriously influenced in form and content by progressive educational ideas (for example by allowing for teacher-initiated syllabuses, and the acceptance of oral work and collected course work as parts of the exam). The proposed merging of O level and CSE into a common sixteen plus exam[4] amounts to an attempted reconciliation of the three lobbies we have identified. The hybrid that may result would undoubtedly be a better exam than traditional O level, but, whatever formula is devised to avoid the surgical crudity of a single pass/fail line, the use of education as a social divider is not seriously put at risk; for as the progressives gradually widen the notion of human talent so that larger numbers of people are seen to have some, and as the numbers possessing approved pieces of paper gradually increase, so employers, professions and higher education institutions increase the number and level of pieces of paper they require.[5] This is the general trend although some higher educational institutions, notably the Open University, are trying to counter it to a greater or lesser degree.

What are the progressives' objections to selection? Principally that it is taking place in a hierarchical society, so that its function in identifying aptitudes and skills is inseparable from its function in allocating unequal 'life chances'.[6] If the reward and status of all jobs in society were approximately equal, selection might be simply an attempt to help people find the jobs they would do best and help employers find the people they need most. There would remain profound objections; the objection, for example, to the assumption that an individual is fitted by nature for only one kind of job, or that the community gets best value out of the individual if he permanently specializes. Would not a variety of different kinds of job both increase personal satisfaction and give the individual a practical grasp of complementary aspects of society, thus greatly increasing his understanding of the function of any one specialism? And of course the equalization of earned reward would not in itself solve the problems of unearned income, exploitation and power. People at the top don't need A levels – only those half way up. Nevertheless the objections to selection would be dramatically reduced. Till such time, the value of selection and attainment testing will remain highly ambivalent despite its claim to be a progressive instrument.

IQ AND IDEOLOGY

Manpower is rarely visible as a direct participant in the debate on educational testing. But its presence can be inferred, again, from the patronage which various schools of thought attract. The most famous educational test is probably the IQ. This is a standardized test, claiming to detect innate mental qualities, and mostly used for selection. IQ lives on despite years of professional criticism not simply because of its remaining academic devotees – fixated on its reliability, oblivious to its narrowness[7] – but because of its ideological convenience. Thus, in an article on racial difference:

Where the average IQ of a group is about 85, there are around 16 per cent with IQs lower than 70 and this is the range in which people tend to be not sufficiently competent to be worth employing in an advanced industrial society. Thus a group with a low intelligence level is a burden for the rest of the population to carry.[8]

By a blatant double twist, whatever it is that IQ measures is instantly translated into the only criterion of employability and then employability into the sole criterion of human worth. Originality, courage, imagination, value judgement, kindness, creativity, as well as a great many other attributes that we would normally consider a part of intelligence, just don't get a look-in.

What is really at issue in the debate surrounding the claims of IQ is not the scientific definition of intelligence. Researchers do not approach the problem by attempting to define *what is normally meant by* intelligence but by attempting to validate *what they choose to define as* intelligence. The same applies to 'personality', 'attitudes', 'ability' or 'attainments' in most of the tests using these terms. What is really at issue is our notion of what is important about human beings. 'Objective' methods of assessment are often as conceptually narrow as they are statistically sophisticated, when compared even with our ordinary assessments of each other in the course of everyday encounters. In relation to ourselves and those close to us we all know the differences between the ability to solve crossword puzzles and the ability to solve the problems of living. We know that intellectual capacities fluctuate drastically according to mood and situation, and in our more sensitive moments we are rightly aware that we are seeing only a small part of those we confront. Yet when it comes to education, where one would have expected such imagination and flexibility to be essential, we often submerge this rich repertoire of insights in rigid and simplified measures.

The existence of a multiplicity of other human variables does not necessarily render such measures as IQ inaccurate or non-'objective' in their own terms. It only shows the limitations of the relevance of IQ to problem solving capacities in the wide sense in which real situations, including work situations, make their demands on us. The usefulness of tests depends on the discretion with which they are interpreted. Once their limitations are forgotten they may become worse than useless. Reservations in the small print are not enough. Our trust in 'objective' measures needs to be tempered by a rich sensibility towards the full complexity of human beings. If this makes the overall ranking of human beings highly dubious, so much the worse for the principle of hierarchy. The quality of life of a society depends on the contribution of the entire community, not just on the capabilities of an élite.

TESTING OF OBJECTIVES

The ambivalent promise of curriculum evaluation as an instrument for rationalizing education comes from the fact that it is forged in the same behaviourist laboratory that produces testing for selection and attainment. Teachers are recommended to apply 'objective' test technique in the planning and execution of all courses. Briefly, the technique consists of writing down objectives for each class of pupils in such a way that the exact degree to which they have attained these objectives can be concretely tested before and after each course of teaching; and the course itself would be designed closely around the specified objectives. Clearly this approach is based on an image of knowledge as a commodity the supply of which is at the teacher's command; and a pupil's level of attainment at any given time is seen as constituting a precise and ascertainable stage along a single path of knowledge mastery known to the expert in advance.

The reasoning is clear : without tests how is anyone to know just what has and what has not been learnt? Undoubtedly the spread of this reasoning is exposing extensive irrationality in traditional education which, in retrospect, appears to have been extraordinarily hazy about its purposes and effects. Evaluation methods are unquestionably a useful means of exposing the irrationality of traditional education *in its own terms* – the ingestion of prescribed knowledge – and of structuring objectives and courses in that proportion of the curriculum in which the teacher must legitimately know beforehand exactly what the children are to learn. But just what proportion of the curriculum this should be is a matter of dispute. In practice many of the objectives of education are generated in the very confrontation of teacher and taught, just as the 'objectives' of an ordinary conversation are.

On the one hand curriculum evaluation is an attempt to rationalize this process of identifying objectives. On the other hand it has its roots in a technological ethos and does not recognize the subtlety, complexity and flexibility of social interactions, including those in the classroom – how quickly, perhaps subconsciously, a teacher may process all sorts of cues and accordingly modify his goals or methods on the instant. Practitioners of curriculum evaluation call it a 'technology' and its paradigms of educational objectives are invariably worked out first in mathematical or scientific subject matter and then extrapolated to other subjects. The fact that it is ill adapted to serve some of those subjects is revealed by the way in which some of its central terminology fails to cover meanings understood by the same phraseology in those other subjects. Thus to the curriculum technologists 'evaluation' essentially means measurement, whereas in the humanities it means judgement by reference to personal, moral or social values – a distinctly non-measuring activity. And the 'affective' category of the technologists is used to cover objectives such as imaginativeness and creativity because these do not involve cognitive learning of a kind which teachers can fully prestructure; but humanities teachers would argue that imaginativeness and creativity have vital cognitive functions because they involve the organization of perceptions.[9]

Tests are essentially an adjunct to the impressionistic and intuitive judgements of good teaching, not a substitute for them. Even the best tests can never be as subtle, complex, rapid and flexible as the continual intuitive assessment acts made by a good teacher in the course of ordinary teaching.[10] A teacher may modify his goals several times in a lesson, for individual pupils or groups, in the light of feedback obtained and interpreted on the spot, including pupil initiatives. (In chapter 6 we called such modifications 'fruitful deviations'.) Research and theory on objectives, however, tend to ignore the more informal kinds of feedback, and particularly the possibility of pupil initiatives which might result, beneficially, in a change of direction for the lesson or course.

It is not sufficiently appreciated that test technique and the formal ordering of objectives represent the rationalization of a process already 'invisibly' carried out by good teachers. The major difference is that while formal testing and writing of objectives can only practicably be carried out at fairly substantial intervals, the teacher's intuitive assessments are a recurrent part of teaching itself. If formal test technique were to become mandatory without sufficient recognition that the same process goes on in a more fluid, less visible, way all the time, it could become an impediment to good teaching rather than a help. It might at times appear that, according to a formal plan, one had gone 'off course', and one might be unable to justify in the 'correct' terminology a complex intuitive process, when in reality one had succeeded in assimilating, perhaps to a large degree subconsciously, a whole series of cues from pupils, and in changing course appropriately.

THE TEST SITUATION

In its present state of development, test technique assumes a complete foreknowledge on the part of the teacher of what is to be learned; it assumes also the divisibility of this content into convenient testable units or 'items'. In some subjects at least, this goes right against the grain of the subject matter. Multiple-choice-type tests confine the mental activity of the pupil to prearranged paths in a way that is liable to cause loss of interest, of motivation and therefore of attainment. The 'objectivity' of such tests is achieved only by reducing the part played by the pupil to a mere tick or cross – which may or may not have elaborate thought processes behind it, but certainly does not *express* those thought processes. In addition, the tests are rarely as objective as they at first appear. Success may depend on happening to guess the particular rationale behind the constructing of the item, since an alternative but equally legitimate rationale would frequently produce a different correct answer.

The fundamental problem with testing is not the danger of inaccuracy in the tests, which can only be demonstrated to the extent that you can develop a new test to show up the failure of the old, but lies in what has been excluded by designing the test so as to isolate measurable factors. Because the tester, in his quest for objectivity, has carefully narrowed his focus onto a particular limited kind of attainment, he tends to put himself into a position where he can no longer appreciate the great variety of possible reasons why a pupil should do badly on a test *other* than lack of the specific thing being tested. Labov[11] has discussed the dramatic improvement in articulacy that can be demonstrated when the test situation is altered – when, for example, instead of the usual middle class, formal tester, the test is conducted by an informal, working class tester who starts by deliberately showing that he will make no attempt to dominate the pupil and that there are to be no linguistic taboos such as that against swearing. Analogous impediments are probably operative all the time in test situations. If some pupils are alienated by school life or by some aspects of it, quite obviously they are not going to try their best in test situations, which inevitably repeat all the cultural and atmospheric features of the school situation. And if some of the subjects are not trying their best, the results are meaningless. Herbert Kohl recounts how a girl pupil with a very low reading score amazed him by reading everything on his desk fluently. He asked how it was that she could read so well yet had such a low reading score. ' "I wouldn't read for those teachers. Listen—". Alice picked up a book and stumbled through several paragraphs. She paused, stuttered, committed omissions and reversals, i.e. read on a low third-grade level. Then she looked at my astonished face and burst out laughing.'[12]

The real test situation faced by the pupil is never the

one contained *in* the test – it is the one created by the requirement to *do* the test. The pupil may use as much problem-solving ability and as much intelligence in evading demands made on him as in attempting to fulfil those demands. Pupils who do fulfil demands are evidently able to do so. But pupils who do not are not necessarily unable. 'Ability' is therefore not necessarily what distinguishes them.

Limitations of this kind are not news to educational test constructors and researchers. Indeed, it is part of their professional virtue to point them out. But just as the ingenuousness of the academics does not alter the use that employers make of academic qualifications, so the pious cautionary footnotes and disclaimers of test constructors[13] do not materially impede the use of their tests to legitimize educational, occupational and social stratification.

CONTEXT AND LIMITATIONS OF TESTING

What is it that enables us to interpret tests sensibly, to place their findings in the context of real human complexity? Nothing other than our sensibility towards everything about human beings which is *not* reflected in the tests. Everything, that is, which we know from our personal relationships, our ordinary observations, our more varied reading, our reflections and our intuitions. Far from 'objective' testing rendering these more informal kinds of knowledge superfluous, it is entirely dependent on them for its hypotheses, its instruments and its interpretations alike. Interpretations of research data will always be unconvincing where alternative explanations of the observed phenomena have not been considered and eliminated. The ability to posit alternative explanations of educational facts or processes depends on nothing more 'objective' than general human sensibility and imagination. Technological sophistication is not enough. If educational and other forms of social research often fail to satisfy or convince, the key fault lies not in particular aspects of test technique but in the poverty of the concept *human being* underlying so much of the work in this field.

Since psychology has been dominated by behaviourism, renouncing interest in the subjective dimensions of experience, it has been, by comparison with even the common discourse of our culture, a painfully narrow area. Surprisingly, in view of the fact that the historical roots of psychology and sociology are in the literary and philosophical tradition, we find in most behaviouristic research in these subjects a neglect of verbal sophistication, and a failure to appreciate that this can ruin research or testing just as surely as statistical error. It may be that in its bid for scientific status, behaviourism has deliberately abstracted itself from the verbal and conceptual precision characteristic of (the best work in) the humanities, thus disdaining that expertise which alone could ensure validity in its own inescapably verbal instruments and interpretations.

It is elementary in the 'verbal' disciplines that the meaning of words and the weight to be attached to them depends on the context in which they appear. In the attitude and personality questionnaires which form the 'affective' side of educational testing and research, phrases are systematically stripped of context in order that they can be made into measurable 'items'. The statistical correlations which can then be demonstrated between various people's endorsements of these enfeebled fragments of language are frequently meaningless. The number of people who tick 'strongly agree' or 'slightly disagree' when presented with an isolated value statement may correspond to little more than the surface popularity or currency of certain phraseology in a particular pocket of our culture at a particular historical moment. (This is apart from identifiable ambiguities of linguistic denotation which may frequently be found on close inspection of test or research instruments.)

Paradoxically enough, most behavioural instruments tell us little about behaviour. And because they fail to face squarely their dependence on the nature of language, they remain at the mercy of the primitive illusion that words represent facts. There is a failure to recognize that an idea or statement is not a *reproduction* of reality but an instrument for *engaging with* or *operating on* reality in some way. There is of course a representational element in all thought but thought is built on the felt presence of far more than is actually represented in itself. It operates on or in a context which is felt and known without being represented, and which is therefore not observable in individual statements – but which is felt and known differently by different people.

An example of the neglect of context in educational research interpretation is the importance that has been attached by teacher educators to the finding that a key variable in educational effectiveness is 'the attitude of the teacher'. From this it is deduced that the job of teacher educators is to inculcate certain attitudes in tomorow's teachers. Researchers then design further instruments to test whether the attitudes of teacher students are influenced by their courses. It is instantaneously forgotten that attitudes could only have been of interest in the first place in so far as they could be taken to reflect what teachers actually said or did in the classroom, and that they do not necessarily mean the same thing once the situation in which they first appeared is changed. Thus in the college environment, 'attitudes', isolated from the conditions in which they are intended to operate, become purely a matter of producing the right form of words in an essay, seminar or attitude test. The relation of this to real behaviour in the stressful situation of school is unknown. Hence the rapid changes of attitude which many new teachers are said to undergo when they are plunged into the school situation. Hence, equally, the adoption of teaching 'behaviours' which may contradict even attitudes still nominally held.

In reality attitudes on such questions as whether children ought to be taught in this or that way or whether schools ought to have these, those or the other objectives are likely to have at least four dimensions, any or all of which can be present simultaneously, or any of which may be absent: they are *directives* of behaviour – things the individual has worked out to guide his own actions (without necessarily

being able to fulfil them); they are *reflections* of behaviour
– ways that the individual explains to himself or justifies
actions that he has found himself taking; they are *cover-ups*
of behaviour – ways that the individual disguises from
himself or others, or compensates for, *contrary* tendencies
in his behaviour; and they are *purely verbal* – reflections
of reasoning, or simply of a climate of opinion unmediated
by individual reasoning, having no particular relation to
the individual's behaviour. The last category would include
attitudes adopted to conform with what those in authority
over you appear to want to hear.

In general, educational technology assumes attitudes to
be simply indicators of intentional or habitual behaviour.
It systematically screens out that feature of thought which
is most distinctively human – its ambivalence. Thought can
only be measured by reducing it to an aspect of itself. In
its full and characteristic complexity it can only be *judged*
– evaluated in the *non*-technological sense – and only by
other, equally 'non-objective' thought. Educational tests are
a useful tool *at some points* in the judging process. As a
substitute for that process they can be a disaster.

The battle between different psychological theories is a
battle between different conceptions of what man *is*. And
what we are faced with in the submission of educational
theory to behaviourism is a systematic reduction of the
concept of man. This is not a reduction of man himself;
his complexity is irreducible. The danger, however, is that
an education modelled on too shallow a picture of what
man is will be disastrously inadequate to equip men's minds
to cope with that society which man himself, in his complexity, has made and been made by.

If curriculum evaluation can emerge from its rather
narrow origins and develop in such a way as to accommodate more imaginative aims it could be a valuable progressive instrument. Otherwise it will remain principally
an adjunct to selection and stratification. Its main limitation
is its reliance on the teacher's knowing in advance of a
course exactly what the pupils are to get out of it. This is
a reasonable presupposition in so far as education is initia-

tion into a secure body of knowledge which the teacher has thoroughly mastered and the value and significance of which is unaffected by the experience, values and self-awareness of those who must now master it in turn. But education, particularly in the humanities and social sciences, is in large measure, and rightly so, an activity in which received knowledge is revaluated in the very process of being assimilated. For this process the teacher requires an expertise based on very different assumptions from those governing 'educational technology'.

NOTES

[1] See for example D. Nuttall and A. Wilmott, *British Examinations, Techniques of Analysis* (Slough, NFER, 1972).

[2] See E. Stones, *An Introduction to Educational Psychology* (London, Methuen, 1966), pp. 263ff.

[3] There are an increasing number of books designed to explain and advocate curriculum evaluation techniques for schools. Examples are S. Wiseman and D. Pidgeon, *Curriculum Evaluation* (Slough, NFER, 1970) and J. F. Kerr (ed.), *Changing the Curriculum* (London, University of London Press, 1967). The most exhaustive attempt to provide a model for teaching objectives which can be 'behaviourally' tested, and probably the most influential book in the field, is B. S. Bloom *et al.*, *Taxonomy of Educational Objectives, Handbook I, The Cognitive Domain* (London, Longmans Green, 1956).

[4] See the review of Schools Council Work on these and related proposals, 'Butler and Briault agree on new sixth form examinations', *The Times Educational Supplement* (4 May 1973).

[5] Asa Briggs and A. G. Watts, 'Are your A-levels really necessary?', *The Sunday Times Magazine* (7 October 1973), show how the starting qualifications required by various

professions have increased over recent years.

[6] The relative advantages, in terms of earnings and prospects, of various educational qualifications are detailed in Office of Population Censuses and Surveys, Social Survey Division, *The General Household Survey, Introductory Report* (London, HMSO, 1973). This was summarized by John Gretton, 'What it's all for', *The Times Educational Supplement* (20 July 1973).

[7] H. J. Eysenck, in 'A better understanding of IQ and the myths surrounding it', *The Times Educational Supplement* (18 May 1973), reports the 'exciting' news that IQ correlates with simple neurological measures like eye-flicker. Instead of showing, as he claims, that the definition of intelligence is becoming more and more scientific, this only shows that IQ is even closer to reflex actions than to what we normally mean by intelligence.

[8] Richard Lynn, 'Intelligence in black and white', *Daily Telegraph* (20 May 1972).

[9] See for example Henry B. Maloney (ed.), *Accountability and the Teaching of English* (Urbana, Ill., National Council of Teachers of English, 1972).

[10] M. Cameron-Jones and A. Morrison, 'Teachers' assessments of their pupils' in G. Chanan (ed.), *Towards a Science of Teaching* (Slough, NFER, 1973), attempt a complete categorization of teachers' observable 'assessment acts' in the course of teaching.

[11] W. Labov, 'The logic of nonstandard English', in P. P. Giglioli (ed.), *Language and Social Context* (Harmondsworth, Penguin, 1972).

[12] Herbert Kohl, *36 Children* (Harmondsworth, Penguin Education Special, 1972), pp. 189-90.

[13] On behalf of educational testers in general, David C. McClelland laments in a critical article that 'the public took us more seriously than we did ourselves'. 'Testing for competence rather than "intelligence"', *American Psychologist*, 28 (1) (1973) (published by the American Psychological Association Inc., Washington DC).

Chapter 8

Cultural revaluation

Cultural revaluation does not mean merely new interpretations of art and literature. If traditional culture fails to carry conviction with many of today's teachers and pupils it is because it seems to have been relegated to a department of its own, highly revered in theory, sometimes invoked as an ultimate reference point for *personal* behaviour and experience, virtually ignored as a source of values for policies and practices in society as a whole.

Our emerging culture will distinguish itself from all former dominant cultures by not being tailored to the interests or glorification of a ruling class nor being an instrument at the disposal of priestly castes or academic experts. It will need to be able to inspire values relevant to questions like: how can members of hitherto exploited classes or nations become self-determining? How can classes or societies which hitherto saw themselves as 'humanity', and the alien as expendable, exploitable or barbarian, learn to take nourishment from diversity? What forms should personal fulfilment take when liberated from the notion that pleasure and achievement consist in being better, happier, richer or more powerful that others? What forms should communal fulfilment take when liberated from the notion that social good consists in the creation of ever more sophisticated material needs and a permanently escalating exploitation of natural resources?

There can be no illusion that culture alone (like education alone) could *solve* questions like how to end exploitation, how to prevent the depletion of world resources, how to reconcile hostile factions, and so forth. Culture has more to do with activating values and modes of perception *favourable* to the solutions of problems than with the prescription of specific solutions. But the role of culture in making solutions firstly conceivable and secondly acceptable is clearly immense; and its role in deepening the way we experience those problems is paramount. Culture cannot be adequately explained as a 'superstructure' on an 'economic base' (the Marxist formula). Despite the inevitable ideological element in culture, the fact that the strength of this element varies, and often in inverse proportion to the quality of the work of art (or whatever) shows that the phenomenon of culture as such cannot be wholly accounted for or evaluated by ideological or economic determinants.

In order to be able to illuminate such questions the new culture will have to be built on respect for the autonomy of all human beings. That educationists are still far off from appreciating this need is shown by its conspicuous neglect in most discussions of educational aims:

The attention of children should be directed towards their duties and rights as citizens, towards the responsibilities involved in marriage and bringing up a family, and towards opportunities for service to the neighbourhood and to a wider society. It is also necessary to prepare them for responsible adult personal relationships by way of personal manners, poise and courtesy and by developing their capacity for personal relationships and sympathetic response to persons of the same and of different traditions and cultures.... Pupils should be prepared in order to cope with the circumstances of work in a modern industrial society. This would involve particular regard for: (a) the speed of technological change and the

accompanying shifts in the balance of work and leisure,
(b) the need to accustom them gradually to the requirements of the world of work, (c) training in the practical
complexities of adult life, e.g. money management, hire
purchase, housing.[1]

Of course, everyone would agree with many of these
prescriptions. But what is so unsatisfactory about formula-
tions of this kind is not simply the manifest wish that
pupils should fit in with society as it is, disturbing it as
little as possible, but the apparent bland belief that society
can be fitted in with – that it is in itself coherent and fair;
that reality is negotiable by simply attaining a maturity in
the prescribed terms. One would get no inkling from this
statement that personal relationships or working situations
are continual areas of conflict, both of interests and values.
There is no attention to the fact that conflict, in oneself
and between self and others, is one of the most fundamental
human experiences – the very one, indeed, that makes values
necessary. There is no hint of the fact that 'the speed of
technological change' is itself a cause for alarm; or that
its benefits, including 'shifts in the balance of work and
leisure', are not automatically and equitably passed on but
have to be fought for. There is no felt need to warn young
people that 'the requirements of the world of work' are
frequently dehumanizing and would need to be resisted by
any self-respecting human being; or to alert them to the
fact that society coheres as much by resistance to conventional norms as by conformity to them. And there is no
apparent attachment of importance to the existential problems of autonomy which underlie all values in society –
how to structure time, how to attribute relative value to
different experiences, how to cultivate extended personal
memory, how to cope with grief, how to enjoy.

Yet it must not be thought that 'progressive' educational
reasoning generally gives, by contrast, proper recognition
to the element of people's autonomy in shaping their
future. Man the chooser is often lost in the image of inexorable social change and impersonal progress. 'Reality'

is given a sparkling new brand image, but we're still being told that it's impervious to our influence and we just have to fit in with it:

> In the decades to come we shall have to reckon with an accelerated process of change in many fields, triggered off by innovations in electronics and computer technology.... This growth will be accompanied by a rise in individual standards of living. But a problem arising from this kind of change is the 'culture lag', found not only in institutions, e.g. the education system, but also in personal attitudes and values, which derive from a state of society where the external determinants of technology, economics and institutions were different.... The new technology will require many people ... to undergo total retraining.[2]

The dynamism of this vision distracts attention from its bleakness. Culture, values and attitudes – the entire mind of man – are seen as mere reflections of particular technological conditions. There is no room for values to be what they really are – people's judgements of whatever affects them by their effect on themselves as human beings. If social progress is to have any real meaning technology must be judged by its effect on us, not we by our attitude to technology!

Correspondingly, the easy promise of higher living standards is made without any concrete thought about, firstly, what people have to do in order to obtain these higher standards, and secondly just what makes a living standard 'higher'. When we detach standard of living from autonomy we end up with a criterion which is external to man. To see social change as something that happens to man irrespective of his wish or decision (rather than as a process which effects his wishes and decisions in frequently unforeseen ways which he must then judge afresh) is to encourage resignation to the uncontrollable – which may then indeed become uncontrollable.

Our values are permeated by an abstract idea of change or progress, instead of a progressively refined image of the condition we want to progress *to*. In the deification of the idea of progress man is distracted from his capacity for fulfilment in this world just as much as he was in the middle ages by the idea of the hereafter. It deflects him in the first place from the relatively short-term motivations which are the real springs of *chosen* social change, and in the second place from the existential problem of living one's own life in one's own lifetime. Fixation on too abstract a concept of progress may deflect attention from both life and death. It is one way of avoiding the consciousness of death (since our lives are seen as primarily contributing to some ideal state to be enjoyed by future generations, without our seeing that those generations are going to live through essentially the same suspended consciousness that we do now) and hence of cheating ourselves of the necessary framework for the full valuing of life.

The attack on human autonomy, representing perhaps a fear of freedom, has a wardrobe which can make it respectable in any political company. Where the conservative sees society statically, as if values culled from the past could be applied to our own times without reinterpretation, and the progressive sees a future of endless change, evolutionary and impersonal, the radical is tempted to seek not endless but 'total' change – to believe that at the orgasmic moment of revolution, changes will occur which so alter our idea of what is possible that there is no point in trying to make any provision for them now. A simplified dialectical model permits the assertion that pure opposition is all that is needed to create the future synthesis out of the present. Yet there is, of course, no such thing as a total qualitative break in history, even in a revolution – and if there were it would become meaningless to those who experienced it, since it implies a break in their consciousness as absolute as that in social organization. In those who insist on the need for *total* change we must assume either that there are unexamined mental reservations, or a concealed attraction to oblivion.

Respect for autonomy means, in education, recognition for the fact that pupils, like all of us, are already actively engaged in the refashioning of a culture. We remarked at the end of chapter 4 that real sources of original thought are impossible to ascertain. The conventional image of the original thinker is of someone who adds a new bit on top of existing thought, a bit which may or may not eventually result in the reinterpretation of existing thought. But new forms of thought do not necessarily manifest themselves first as additions to an existing store of knowledge which has already been mastered. They may very well manifest themselves first as disagreements with some aspect or other of the existing store of knowledge, and when they are incipient they are not likely to be fully articulate and cogent. When pupils show their rejection of some aspect of received knowledge (mediated, we must always remember, by a single, fallible teacher) they are almost invariably interpreted as incapable of mastery of it. Yet their rejection may be an incipient form of rational disagreement.

Subjectively, autonomous thought does not experience itself as an attempt at originality but as an attempt to understand given reality, including the reality of received knowledge. It only discovers its degree of autonomy by gradually coming to understand why it *cannot* understand received thought, why the received thought fails to satisfy, fails to illuminate reality. We cannot wholly understand what seems to us untrue because 'understanding', in normal usage, means precisely seeing that the thing *is* true. Only later, with the maturation of the autonomous thought, will the thinker after all come to 'understand' the received thought in the sense of grasping its origins and its function for the person who thinks it is true. Only at this stage could he, if he chose to, demonstrate conventional mastery of the conventional thought. Only now could he 'assume temporarily complete agreement with the statement', as 'objective' testers would have required of him at the start.

Admittedly, when pupils appear to reject 'high' culture – that is, a particular teacher's particular representation of 'high' culture – impatience, prejudice, insecure attachment to crude cultural norms are all possible explanations. Yet it is also possible that the pupil has an incipient disagreement with values or notions attributed to that culture; but this explanation is almost universally ignored.

The emerging culture to which schools should be host and midwife will be a culture of universal humanitarianism. Critics use the term 'humanism' to designate the post-religious culture of the Renaissance and onwards – the culture that includes the beginnings of modern literature, philosophy, science and all that schools are said to hold most dear. But whether this humanism includes or implies universal humanitarianism remains ambivalent. Conservative critics are still not wholly rid of attachment to the class-biased, chauvinist, racist, anti-feminist attitudes that can be found embodied in traditional culture alongside the more enduring humanistic elements. The response of twentieth-century criticism towards the embarrassment of reactionary values in traditional art and literature is essentially a retreat into formalism, a devaluation of subject matter in general. In the past this has been a source of confusion to humanities teachers, who have found themselves trying to argue pupils into appreciating the sonnet form or the construction of metaphors, when these things can have no interest except in relation to the direct representational preoccupations of the poet about love or death; or, on the outing to the art gallery, trying to make out that the fact that it's a naked woman or a dying soldier who is vividly depicted is somehow unimportant compared with the use of perspective or the handling of brushstrokes.[3]

The school of criticism which still provides the basic perspective for the academic valuation of high culture – the school of T. S. Eliot and F. R. Leavis – is one whose humanism is of a passionately abstract-idealist temper. The prevailing notion, the framework for evaluation, is T. S. Eliot's 'ideal order of art'[4] – art as a sublime competitive hierarchy. Ultimately only the degree of greatness of a work of art is of importance, as if all art were trying to do the same thing for the same people, and in a historically static landscape. At the same time, marks of greatness are awarded on values of psychological insight and moral depth. While many of the individual critical insights developed with these criteria are immensely valuable, and do represent substantial contributions to an emerging culture of universal humanitarianism, fixation on the notion of the authority and ideal nature of cultural standards gives rise to the blinkered rigidity of the Black Papers (whose editors edited a 'high culture' literary journal for some time before branching out into educational politics).

The explanation offered by 'high culture' critics for the survival of some works of art while others have perished is their profounder insight into and compassion for the human condition. Yet the original patronage of 'great' art was the patronage of a ruling class which was anything but compassionate in its actual social relations to the mass of people in its own time. Thus the artists we now call great did a job that went much deeper than their patrons had paid for. Starting with the brief of embellishing the life of the court or reflecting the glory of the rich, they not only gradually introduced elements of satire and criticism but depicted their patrons (who were also their subjects) in such a way that everyone could identify with their pleasures and weaknesses, and therefore everyone could come to realize his basic human equality with them. As both artists and patrons became more aware of this process, artists came to be regarded, and to regard themselves, as somewhat abnormal, unconforming people. This contributed to the Romantic image of the artist, which reflects the basic tension not between the artist and *society*, as if society were a unified body of 'normal' people with 'normal' attitudes, but between the artist and his *patronage*. Romanticism was the artist's way of insisting on the importance of this tension, but it was neutralized by the academic solution. The power of art could not be denied, but it could be isolated by accepting its nonconformity and making it into a freak called 'genius', to be idolized but at the same time attributed to individual peculiarities and denied significance as contemporary social criticism. Kicked upstairs, art became Art, something of a substitute for religion, but said to be appreciable by ordinary mortals only a generation or two after its appearance, when its actual context had passed and its 'eternal' qualities began to appear.

The conservative critics are right about the fundamental humanism of great art, but while they can deal safely with its implications for an age now gone they do not see its implications for our own age. They fail to see also that many of those artists who, under the influence of academic criticism, aspire to the mantle of 'high culture' have become, over the past half century, more and more emotionally constipated, self-absorbed and trivial, while much of the vigour and humanism of great art has passed or is passing over into popular culture.

Neither the abdication of judgement glamourized by some progressives nor the secure academic authority assumed by conservatives will really answer the cultural challenge with which we find ourselves faced. The problems posed in our school by the presence of immigrant children are merely the most visible part of this challenge. It is as feeble to speak of the need for immigrants to 'fit in with our way of life' as it is to talk of the need of pupils in general to 'fit in with society'. For we have not got a 'way of life' which we can prescribe in that manner, other than the democratic idea itself, which changes its forms and meaning as new social forces seek expression through it. Democratic principles must certainly provide the structure for our arguments, but cannot themselves settle those arguments. We have the problem of developing a culture adequate to an unprecedented social and global situation; and our cultural history, including our increasing awareness of cultures developed in other societies, forms a store of resources on which we may draw in the fashioning of our values, not a body of readymade values.

Meanwhile what holds us together is a sort of federation of subcultures in various states of tolerance and tension, 'high' culture itself being one of these subcultures rather than *the* culture of our society. Certainly this pluralistic condition will continue, and there will be cross-fertilization. After experiencing the rich cultural diversity of our time it would be torture to arrive after all only at some new monolithic cultural state. But culture is not merely private lifestyle or sublime entertainment. The major social and political problems of our time demand from us continual complex collective value judgements and hence some degree of reconcilability in our values. We might more reasonably, then, speak of the need for immigrants to accommodate to the way of life which is now in the process of creation – a process in which their influence is as valid as ours, and our effort of reaccommodation as necessary as theirs.

That such new syntheses are psychologically possible, and indeed liberating, is shown by hippies who, in contrast to the passive tolerance which is the most that most of us can manage when faced with the unfamiliar, take positive delight in cultural diversity. It would be instructive to study how, in psychological terms, it is possible to transcend one's cultural limitations, or one's hollow attachment to cultural forms which do not actually inspire one's beliefs or behaviour. Clearly some kind of inner confidence is required, which perhaps comes from exercising the sense of creativity, so that one is less dependent on familiar external forms to 'guarantee' reality – and more able to distinguish when they genuinely make reality more manageable.

The values by which we must live in the last quarter of the twentieth century do not exist, then, as a secure body of doctrine which schools can simply hand on, nor will they arrive automatically through some evolutionary adaptation to conditions created by our own technology. They must be consciously created, and are now in the process of creation throughout society; a process in which, if they can rise to it, schools have a vital part to play.

NOTES

[1] From the 'Joint statement of objectives' for comprehensive schools produced by a committee of leading educationists and reproduced as Appendix A in J. M. Ross *et al.*, *A Critical Appraisal of Comprehensive Education* (Slough, NFER, 1972).

[2] Torsten Husén, 'The "learning society" and tomorrow's schools', *London Educational Review*, 1 (2) (1972).

[3] In his television series entitled 'Ways of seeing', John Berger restored the necessary emphasis to subject matter in painting. See John Berger, *Ways of Seeing* (London, BBC and Harmondsworth, Penguin, 1972).

[4] See T. S. Eliot, 'Tradition and the individual talent' (1919) and 'The use of poetry and the use of criticism' (1933) in *Selected Prose*, ed. John Hayward (Harmondsworth, Penguin, 1953).

The authors and publishers would be
interested to hear from anyone who may
wish to comment on the ideas in this
book.

Index

ability, 49, 60, 88, 107, 109, 114
academic disciplines, 5, 29, 65, 68, 73, 86-96
aims, *see objectives*
A levels, 83, 84n, 88, 105
architecture, 83
art,
  works of, 18, 24, 56, 61, 74, 97, 121, 126-8
  teaching of, 52, 126
assessment, 106, 109, *see also* tests
attainment, 23, 49, 81, 89, 106, 109, 116
attitudes, 115, 123

Bantock, G. H., *quoted* 33
Barnes, D., 25
behaviourism, 110, 115-17
Berger, J., 130
Bernstein, B., 36, *quoted* 94-5
Britton, J., 25
Buckman, P., *quoted* 4
Buddhism, 73

Chaplin, C., 47

child-centred teaching, *see* teaching
colleges of education, 15, 36, 116
colloquial speech, 29, 65, 73, 93, 97
comprehensive schools, 51, 82
compulsory education, 4-6
computers, 8
concentration (mental), 74, 93-7
concepts, coordination of, 46, 87-8, 92
control (of pupils), 54-5
convergent thinking, 102-3
creativity, 23, 35-6, 111, 129
CSE, 45, 88, 107
curriculum
  evaluation of, 84, 91, 106, 110-12, 117
  innovations in, 106, *see also* progressive education
  traditional, 5, 53, 84, *see also* traditional education

democracy,
  in schools, 19, 82, 91
  in society, 69, 83, 128
deprivation, 37, 81

deschooling, 1-5, 13, 79
discussion by pupils, 26, 38-46, 101
divergent thinking, 102-3
Downes, A., 21, 69n

educational research, 81-2, 106, 109, 112, 114-16
educational technology, 111, 117, *see also* technology
eleven plus exam, 88, 105
Eliot, T. S., 61, 126
employment, *see* jobs
English, teaching of, 50-1, 59, 126
equality, 50-2, 79, 83, 108
equality of opportunity, 77
evaluation, *see* curriculum
exams, 14, 72, 75, 106, *see also* eleven plus, CSE, O levels, A levels
existentialism, 122, 124
Eysenck, H. J., 119

films, 35, 61
Flanders, N. A., *quoted* 24
Frye, N., *quoted* 28

grammar schools, 51, 83
goals, *see* objectives

Halsey, A. H., 76, *quoted* 84-5n
headmasters, 13
hierarchy (social), 76, 79, 107, 110
'high culture', 48, 55-8, 125-8
higher education, 36, 53, 77, 89-90, 95, 107
Hilsum, S., 20
history 56, 58-9, 61-2, 64-5, 124
teaching of, 51, 59-60
Holly, D., 70
home influence, 22, 87
Hudson, L., 104n
humanism, 126
humanities, 67, 102, 111, 115, 126

Humanities Project (Schools Council) 26
Husén, T., *quoted* 123

ideology, 76, 108-9
Illich, I., 1, 3
immigrants, 128-9
individualized learning, 8
industry, 1, 4, 14, 72, 75-6, 105
in-service training, 15
IQ, 108-9

Jencks, C., 85
Jenning, A. E., 20
jobs (relation of education to), 4, 5, 72, 76-7, 109, 122

Kohl, H., *quoted* 113

Labov, W., 113
language in education, 36-8, 115
law, 98
Leavis, F. R., 126
Lee, D. M., *quoted* 12
left-wing, 13
lessons, 86-93
listening, 24-5, 38
Lynn, R., *quoted* 108-9

McClelland, D. C., *quoted* 119
manpower, 72, 73, 105
Marson, D., 20
Marxism, 10, 69-70n, 121
mass media, 1, 28, 33, 87
Mercer, D., 47
'middle class culture', 32, 48-58, 79
middle class pupils, 22
Morgan, K. P., 104n
multiple choice tests, 112, *see also* tests

Nuttall, D., 118n

objectives (educational), 10, 22-3, 71, 91, 104, 110-12, 121-2
O levels, 88, 105, 107

Open University, 107
originality, 33, 69, 125

permanent education, 3, 6, 83
Peters, R. S., 63-4, 73, *quoted* 63-4, 66
philosophy of education, 63
Pidgeon, D., 47
pop music, 33-5, 61
primary schools, 93
problem-solving, 102, 109, 114
progress (social), 3, 75, 77, 123-4
progressive education, 2, 16, 60-1, 78, 105, 107, 123 *and passim*
psychology, 115, 117, 129

qualifications, 75, 89, 105

radicalism, 10, 57, 124
'Rank and File', 20
rebelliousness (of pupils), 6-7, 50
'relevance' (of education), 29, 78, 95
research, *see* educational research
Romanticism, 58, 127
Rosen, H., 25, 47, *quoted* 26, 99
rules (school), 13, 52, 75
ruling class, 10, 55, 78, 120

science, 102
teaching of, 50-2, 64-5
selection, 106-8, 117
self-expression, 25, 29, 58, 83
Shakespeare, 50, 56-7, 59, 79
social science, 67
standard of living, 79-80, 123
status quo, 12, 79-80
Stones, E., 118n
strikes by schoolchildren, *see* Marson
subjects (at school), 73-4, 86-99, *see also* academic disciplines
subordination, 52-3

Suppes, P., *quoted* 8
syllabus, 17

teachers, 3, 9
attitudes of, 116-17
autonomy of, 9
expectations of, 37-8, 54, 81
function of, 36, 46, 52, 68, 95, 100-1, 111-12
pressures on, 11-16, 35-6, 116
psychology of, 19, 51, 54, 56, 98-9
turnover of, 82, 91
teaching
child-centred, 76, 99, 104, *see also* progressive education
teacher-directed, 18, *see also* traditional education
team teaching, 93
technology, 7-9, 75, 80, 122-3
television, 35, 61
tests (educational), 49, 106, 109-16, 125, *see also* exams
timetable, 13, 16, 75, 87, 92
trade unions, 31
traditional education, 2-7, 27-8, 57, 76, 78, 88, 98, 110, *and passim*
truancy, 6

universities, 15, 32, 86

values, 1, 32, 49-55, 120-3, 129
violence, 24

Watts, A., 84n
Where, *quoted* 5
Wilmott, A., 118n
work, *see* jobs
working class pupils, 1, 4, 9, 49, 60, 76-8 *and passim*
'working class culture', 27, 31-3

Young, M. F. D., 104n

OTHER BOOKS FROM METHUEN

THE OPEN CLASSROOM
A practical guide to a new way of teaching
Herbert R. Kohl

'Let there be no mistake, Mr Kohl is not concerned with the mechanics of teaching, the trivia of methods and aids, but with the underlying attitudes of society.' *The Times Literary Supplement*

EQUAL OPPORTUNITY IN EDUCATION
A reader in social class and educational opportunity
Edited by Harold Silver

'(Harold Silver) has selected adroitly from the continuing and unfinished discussion in order to put together a fair picture of a fascinating element of intellectual and political history.' A. H. Halsey, *The Times Educational Supplement*

SUCCESS AND FAILURE IN THE SECONDARY SCHOOL
An interdisciplinary approach to school achievement
Olive Banks and Douglas Finlayson

An important new consideration of the urgent subject of achievement in secondary schools, based on a four-year study of boys in a grammar, a technical grammar and a comprehensive school.

A SOCIAL HISTORY OF EDUCATION IN ENGLAND
John Lawson and Harold Silver

'. . . it is supremely successful in relating curricular development to social change, and, unlike much English social history, it is history with the ideas put in rather than left out.' Asa Briggs, *New Society*